Catechism of the Christian Faith

A Primer for Young Adults

SAINT PATRICK'S ANGLICAN CHURCH

Traditional Anglican Church of America, Diocese of the Northeast

Written by Dea. Jean Hardouin

Commissioned by Bishop Michael DellaVecchia

Catechism of the Christian Faith: A Primer for Young Adults

Written by Dea. Jean Hardouin

The Jeremiad Christian Homesteaders Gazette, Publisher
www.jeremiadchristianhomesteadersgazette.com

©2025 Michael DellaVecchia and Jean Hardouin

All Rights Reserved. No part of this publication may be reproduced, transmitted, or stored in an information retrieval system in any form or by any means, graphic, mechanical, or electronic, including photocopying, taping, recording, without permission in writing from the publisher.

ISBN: 979-8-9889300-8-2

First Edition, published 2025.

Printed in the United States of America.

7 6 5 4 3 2 1 0

TABLE OF CONTENTS

The Three Major Creeds 1
    The Apostles' Creed 1
    The Nicene Creed 2
    The Athanasian Creed 4

What Must All Christians Believe? 11
    The Bible Is True and Inerrant 11
    God Is a Trinity 19
    God Is the Creator 25
    Jesus Was Begotten, Not Created 31
    The Gospel Is Good News......................... 35
    Sinners Need the Savior 47
    We Confess and Are Forgiven 51
    Jesus Is Our Redeemer 57
    Jesus Was Born of a Virgin 63
    Jesus Is Both Fully God and Fully Man.... 71
    We Are Saved by His Redemption 77
    His Sacrifice Is Perfect and Sufficient 83
    We Must Observe Holy Week................... 87
    He Ascended and Will Return Again 97

The Holy Spirit Indwells Us.................... 101
We Must Be Born Again 109
We Must Receive Sacraments 117
We Are Under Grace, Not the Law 133
We Are Called to a Higher Morality 141
We Must Be Known by Our Good Fruits 159
We Must Fight the Good Fight 165
Faith Is Justified by Works 169
We Go to Church Regularly 175
We Commune With the Saints 179
As Saints, We Must Suffer 193
Heaven and Hell Are Real...................... 203
We Believe in the Life of the World to Come 213

A note to our catechumens:

Although this catechism can benefit all young adult Christians seeking to grow in their Christian faith, the primary purpose of this catechism is to teach you—a *catechumen*[1]—the fundamental doctrines shared by all Christians. These doctrines, if believed to be true and followed with a sincere and obedient heart, will unite you with the Body of Christ.

The Universal Church is conceptualized as a "body"—that is, it is the Body of Christ with Jesus as the Head of the body (Colossians 1:18). We as Christians are knit together with each other in Him. He dwells in us and we in Him, and we, in turn, with each other—not only with those saints who are living on earth now, but also with all the saints in heaven. This is what we mean by the Communion of Saints. Communion is another way of saying unity, and it is this unity that we long for as Christians.

There are many other metaphors describing the united relationship between Christ and

---

[1] A catechumen is a person who has made the decision to become a Christian but is not yet baptized or confirmed.

His Church, such as that He is the Bridegroom and the Church is the bride, and He is the Vine and we are the branches.

In this catechism, the central doctrines that all Christians are duty-bound to believe are presented and discussed, and references from the Bible and various creeds are provided to support every doctrine (note that within the excerpts presented, key concepts are displayed in boldface for your ease of study). Further, the distinctions between Sacred Scripture (the Bible) and Sacred Tradition (the rulings and practices of the Church) will be explained.

This catechism is presented in a somewhat "telegraphic" form—that is, through lists following short introductory paragraphs. The point of this style is to invite opportunities for discussion and further exploration through Bible studies, question-and-answer sessions, and the like. For the purpose of notetaking, each chapter has at least one blank page at the end as well as wide margins. Please do not be shy about writing in your catechism! The idea is for you to use it as an interactive study tool. This catechism uses the King James Version (KJV) of the Bible for excerpted text. The KJV is the standard translation used in all Traditional Anglican Churches.

The purpose of this catechism is to prepare you as a catechumen for Baptism, whereupon you will become part of the family of the Church, and next to prepare you to become confirmed in the Church. By the time of your Confirmation, you will know and understand the Liturgy of the Mass and will become fully incorporated into the life of the Church.

This catechism is only the first step on your journey into Christianity. There is much more to learn beyond the pages of this book. Always feel free to ask questions, but more importantly, never cease to read your Bible and pray to God daily as you walk with Him in this life toward the ultimate goal of enjoying everlasting life with Him. May God bless you richly through the words you will be studying here.

The Three Major Creeds

The Apostles' Creed

I BELIEVE in God the Father Almighty, Maker of heaven and earth:

And in Jesus Christ his only Son our Lord: Who was conceived by the Holy Ghost, Born of the Virgin Mary: Suffered under Pontius Pilate, Was crucified, dead, and buried: He descended into hell; The third day he rose again from the dead: He ascended into heaven, And sitteth on the right hand of God the Father Almighty: From thence he shall come to Judge the quick and the dead.

I believe in the Holy Ghost: The holy Catholic Church; The Communion of Saints: The Forgiveness of sins: The Resurrection of the body: And the Life everlasting. Amen. [2]

---

[2] The Apostles' Creed is a short-form creed generally used in the religious instruction of younger children. It was developed sometime between the fourth and eighth centuries and is believed to reflect the teachings of the Apostles.

The Nicene Creed

I BELIEVE in one God the Father Almighty, Maker of heaven and earth, And of all things visible and invisible:

And in one Lord Jesus Christ, the only-begotten Son of God; Begotten of his Father before all worlds, God of God, Light of Light, Very God of very God; Begotten, not made; Being of one substance with the Father; By whom all things were made: Who for us men and for our salvation came down from heaven, And was incarnate by the Holy Ghost of the Virgin Mary, And was made man: And was crucified also for us under Pontius Pilate; He suffered and was buried: And the third day lie rose again according to the Scriptures: And ascended into heaven, And sitteth on the right hand of the Father: And he shall come again, with glory, to judge both the quick and the dead; Whose kingdom, shall have no end.

And I believe in the Holy Ghost, The Lord, and Giver of Life, Who proceedeth from the Father and the Son; Who with the Father and the Son together is worshipped and glorified; Who spake by the Prophets: And I believe one Catholic and Apostolic Church: I acknowledge one Baptism for the remission of sins: And I look for the Resurrection of the dead: And the Life of the world to come. Amen. [3]

---

[3] The Nicene Creed is included in our 1928 Book of Common Prayer, which we use for the Daily Office, the Sunday Mass, and other celebrations in the life of the Traditional Anglican Church. The Nicene Creed is slightly longer than the Apostles' Creed, but unlike the Apostles' creed it does not include mention of Jesus descending into hell. Jesus's descent into hell is a very important concept in Christianity, however, so this shows that we must look at all the major creeds together as rightful expressions of the whole Christian faith. This is why this catechism includes the Apostles' Creed and the Athanasian Creed in addition to the much more familiar Nicene Creed.

The Nicene Creed was formulated at the First Council of Nicaea in 325 A.D. to affirm orthodox Christian teaching against a host of heresies, establishing the monotheism of the Trinity, the true nature of Jesus Christ (fully God and fully man), and the divinity of the Holy Spirit among other important truths.

The Athanasian Creed

WHOSOEVER will be saved: before all things it is necessary that he hold the Catholic Faith.

Which Faith except every one do keep whole and undefiled: without doubt he shall perish everlastingly.

And the Catholic Faith is this: That we worship one God in Trinity, and Trinity in Unity;

Neither confounding the Persons: nor dividing the Substance.

For there is one Person of the Father, another of the Son: and another of the Holy Ghost.

But the Godhead of the Father, of the Son, and of the Holy Ghost, is all one: the Glory equal, the Majesty co-eternal.

Such as the Father is, such is the Son: and such is the Holy Ghost.

The Father uncreate, the Son uncreate: and the Holy Ghost uncreate.

The Father incomprehensible, the Son incomprehensible: and the Holy Ghost incomprehensible.

The Father eternal, the Son eternal: and the Holy Ghost eternal.

And yet they are not three eternals: but one eternal.

As also there are not three incomprehensibles, nor three uncreated: but one uncreated, and one incomprehensible.

So likewise the Father is Almighty, the Son Almighty: and the Holy Ghost Almighty.

And yet they are not three Almighties: but one Almighty.

So the Father is God, the Son is God: and the Holy Ghost is God.

And yet they are not three Gods: but one God.

So likewise the Father is Lord, the Son Lord: and the Holy Ghost Lord.

And yet not three Lords: but one Lord.

For like as we are compelled by the Christian verity: to acknowledge every Person by himself to be God and Lord;

So are we forbidden by the Catholic Religion: to say there be three Gods, or three Lords.

The Father is made of none: neither created, nor begotten.

The Son is of the Father alone: not made, nor created, but begotten.

The Holy Ghost is of the Father and of the Son: neither made, nor created, nor begotten, but proceeding.

So there is one Father, not three Fathers; one Son, not three Sons: one Holy Ghost, not three Holy Ghosts.

And in this Trinity none is afore, or after other: none is greater, or less than another;

But the whole three Persons are co-eternal together: and co-equal.

So that in all things, as is aforesaid: the Unity in Trinity, and the Trinity in Unity is to be worshipped.

He therefore that will be saved: must thus think of the Trinity.

Furthermore it is necessary to everlasting salvation: that he also believe rightly the Incarnation of our Lord Jesus Christ.

For the right Faith is that we believe and confess: that our Lord Jesus Christ, the Son of God, is God and Man;

God, of the Substance of the Father, begotten before the worlds: and Man, of the Substance of his Mother, born in the world;

Perfect God, and Perfect Man: of a reasonable soul and human flesh subsisting;

Equal to the Father, as touching his Godhead: and inferior to the Father, as touching his Manhood.

Who although he be God and Man: yet he is not two, but one Christ;

One, not by conversion of the Godhead into flesh: but by taking of the Manhood into God;

One altogether, not by confusion of Substance: but by unity of Person.

For as the reasonable soul and flesh is one man: so God and Man is one Christ.

Who suffered for our salvation: descended into hell, rose again the third day from the dead.

He ascended into heaven, he sitteth on the right hand of the Father, God Almighty: from whence he shall come to judge the quick and the dead.

At whose coming all men shall rise again with their bodies: and shall give account for their own works.

And they that have done good shall go into life everlasting: and they that have done evil into everlasting fire.

This is the Catholic Faith: which except a man believe faithfully, he cannot be saved.

Glory be to the Father, and to the Son: and to the Holy Ghost;

As it was in the beginning, is now, and ever shall be: world without end. Amen.[4]

---

[4] Attributed to St. Athanasius, but probably not written by him, the Athanasian Creed is intended to establish the truth of the Trinity and to repudiate the Arian heresy. The Arian heresy held that Jesus was a created being and not divine—an abominable blasphemy. Modern-day Arian heretics include Jehovah's Witnesses and other similar groups who deny the Trinity and hence deny the divinity of Christ.

The Athanasian Creed is occasionally used in some Western Christian churches on special occasions and is important to know and understand, even if not recited on a regular basis.

NOTES:

NOTES:

What Must All Christians Believe?

The Bible Is True and Inerrant

All the statements of faith contained within the Christian creeds listed in the previous chapter are derived from the Bible, which we will alternately refer to from time to time throughout this catechism as the Holy Scriptures or Sacred Scripture—all meaning the same thing.

Because the primary source of our knowledge of the Christian faith comes from the Holy Scriptures, it stands to reason that we must believe in the integrity and truth of these Scriptures. Therefore, in order to become a believer in Christ and an adherent of the Christian faith, all Christians must believe that:

- The Holy Scriptures consist of both the Old Testament (books written before the Incarnation of Christ) and the New Testament (books written after the Incarnation of Christ).

- The Holy Scriptures are to be taken in their entirety, with the New Testament fulfilling (not replacing) the Old Testament.
- The Holy Scriptures are inspired by God Himself, in the Person of the Holy Ghost (also known as the Holy Spirit, the third Person of the Trinity), who spoke through the prophets in the Old Testament and by the Apostles in the New Testament.
  - In the **Nicene Creed** we confess: "I believe in the Holy Ghost, The Lord, and Giver of Live, Who proceedeth from the Father and the Son; Who with the Father and the Son together is worshipped and glorified; **Who spake by the Prophets.**"
- The Holy Scriptures are true and without error (known as the doctrine of Biblical Inerrancy) and different verses of the Bible can be used to support each other and interpret meanings. However, it is the Church that provides the ultimate context and interpretation, because the Bible cannot be subject to "private interpretation"—if the Church does not

give context and interpretation, people will come up with heterodox ideas, and that is how heresies, schisms, and Christian-seeming cults emerge.

- o **2 Peter 1:** [20] Knowing this first, that **no prophecy of the scripture is of any private interpretation.** [21] For the prophecy came not in old time by the will of man: but holy men of God spake *as they were* moved by the Holy Ghost.
- o The Church is given the power to "bind and loose" and that means the Church has the authority to teach and interpret the words of the Bible:
  Matthew 18: [18] Verily I say unto you, Whatsoever ye shall bind on earth shall be bound in heaven: and whatsoever ye shall loose on earth shall be loosed in heaven.
- o It is the responsibility of the Church to teach so that people may believe:
  Romans 10: [14] How then shall they call on him in whom they have not believed? and how shall they believe in him of whom

they have not heard? and how shall they hear without a preacher? ¹⁵ And **how shall they preach, except they be sent?** as it is written, How beautiful are the feet of them that preach the gospel of peace, and bring glad tidings of good things!

- Jesus commands the Apostles (and therefore all Bishops that were to come after them) to "teach all nations," and this is done through the expounding of the Holy Scriptures:

Matthew 28: ¹⁸ And Jesus came and spake unto them, saying, All power is given unto me in heaven and in earth. ¹⁹ **Go ye therefore, and teach all nations,** baptizing them in the name of the Father, and of the Son, and of the Holy Ghost: ²⁰ Teaching them to observe all things whatsoever I have commanded you: and, lo, I am with you always, even unto the end of the world. Amen.

- Sacred Scripture is the primary source of faith, and it has the complete teaching necessary for the Christian faith.
    - **2 Timothy 3:** [16] **All scripture *is* given by inspiration of God,** and *is* profitable for doctrine, for reproof, for correction, for instruction in righteousness: [17] That the man of God may be perfect, thoroughly furnished unto all good works.
- Sacred Tradition holds a position of lesser importance on the one hand, but on the other hand, without Sacred Tradition we would not even have the Holy Scriptures as we know them today. Therefore, Sacred Tradition cannot be ignored but must be followed and respected:
    - **2 Thessalonians 3:** [6] Now we command you, brethren, in the name of our Lord Jesus Christ, that ye withdraw yourselves from every brother that walketh disorderly, and not **after the tradition which he received of us.**

Besides the Canon of Sacred Scripture, from Sacred Tradition we also get things like our Liturgy, which forms our basis of worship; the Liturgical Calendar, which determines when Christian holidays are celebrated; our prayers and creeds, such as are found in the 1928 Book of Common Prayer; our understanding of divine concepts such as the Trinity and the Hypostatic Union; our Sacraments and Sacramentals; definitions of heresy and orthodoxy; the Constitution and Canons of each Church diocese; and the vital decisions made by the Church Fathers affecting the Church Universal, as recorded in the foundational Ecumenical Councils that spanned from 325 A.D. to 787 A.D.

Summary

Since the Holy Scriptures are the primary source of all articles of the Christian faith, we must have confidence in and believe the truth, accuracy, and inerrancy of every book of the Scriptures as wholly inspired by God. At the same time, we must understand that the Holy Scriptures were compiled, interpreted, and expounded upon by the Church Fathers—you can't just interpret the words however you want to, since the Scriptures are not subject to "private interpretation." Therefore, Sacred Tradition (the Church) and Sacred Scripture (the Bible) are held in the highest honor, but of these two, Sacred Scripture has the primary position of honor.

NOTES:

God Is a Trinity

The word "Trinity" does not appear in the Bible, but that does not mean that God is not triune. There are numerous references to the One God as a "plurality" all throughout the Old Testament. While less clear in the Old Testament what Persons constitute the Godhead, in the New Testament the Trinity is clearly revealed: The One God consists of God the Father, God the Son, and God the Holy Spirit.

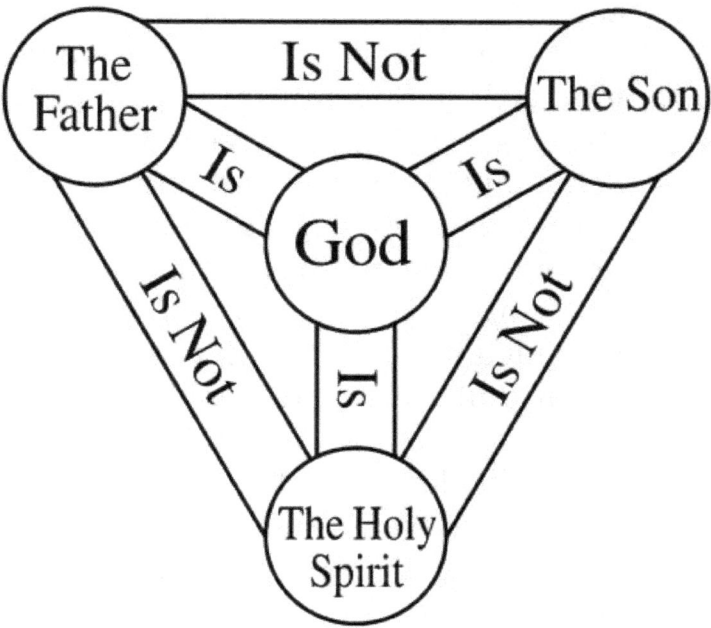

Old Testament

In the Old Testament, God refers to Himself as "us" and even appears once, to Abraham only, as three Persons but one Lord:

- **Genesis 1:** [26] And God said, **Let us** make man in our image, after our likeness: and let them have dominion over the fish of the sea, and over the fowl of the air, and over the cattle, and over all the earth, and over every creeping thing that creepeth upon the earth. [27] So God created man in his own image, in the image of God created he him; male and female created he them.
- **Genesis 11:** [6] And the Lord said, Behold, the people is one, and they have all one language; and this they begin to do: and now nothing will be restrained from them, which they have imagined to do. [7] Go to, **let us** go down, and there confound their language, that they may not understand one another's speech. [8] So the Lord scattered them abroad from thence upon the face of all the earth: and they left off to build the city.
- **Genesis 18:** [1] And the Lord appeared unto him in the plains of Mamre: and

he sat in the tent door in the heat of the day; ²And he lift up his eyes and looked, and, lo, **three men** stood by him: and when he saw them, he ran to meet them from the tent door, and bowed himself toward the ground, ³And said, **My Lord,** if now I have found favour in thy sight, pass not away, I pray thee, from thy servant:
- **Isaiah 6:** ⁸Also I heard the voice of **the Lord,** saying, Whom shall I send, and **who will go for us**? Then said I, Here am I; send me.

New Testament

In the New Testament, which the entire Old Testament points to, God reveals the nature of His plurality, and we learn definitively that the Godhead is a Trinity consisting of God the Father, God the Son, and God the Holy Spirit (aka the Holy Ghost, with "Ghost" merely meaning "Spirit" and therefore incorporeal). There are numerous references to the Father, the Son, and the Holy Spirit being taken to mean the One God. For example:

- **Luke 1:** ³⁵ And the angel answered and said unto her, The Holy Ghost shall come upon thee, and the power of the Highest shall overshadow thee: therefore also that holy thing which shall be born of thee shall be called the Son of God.
- **Matthew 3:** ¹⁶ And Jesus, when he was baptized, went up straightway out of the water: and, lo, the heavens were opened unto him, and he saw the Spirit of God descending like a dove, and lighting upon him: ¹⁷ And lo a voice from heaven, saying, This is my beloved Son, in whom I am well pleased.
- **Matthew 28:** ¹⁸ And Jesus came and spake unto them, saying, All power is given unto me in heaven and in earth. ¹⁹ Go ye therefore, and teach all nations, **baptizing them in the name of the Father, and of the Son, and of the Holy Ghost**: ²⁰ Teaching them to observe all things whatsoever I have commanded you: and, lo, I am with you always, even unto the end of the world. Amen.
- **John 10:** ³⁰ I and my Father are one.

Summary

Although the Holy Trinity in light of our monotheistic faith can seem like a mystery, you can make sense of it this way: You consist of a unique body, a unique soul, and a unique spirit in one being. Your body is not your soul or your spirit; your soul is not your body or your spirit; and your spirit is not your body or your soul. Yet each one of these parts or "persons" can be identified only with **you**—nobody else. Likewise, the Father is not the Son and is not the Holy Ghost; the Son is not the Father and is not the Holy Ghost; and the Holy Ghost is not the Father and is not the Son. And yet, The Father is God, the Son is God, and the Holy Spirit is God: three Persons of the Trinity with different attributes (e.g., the Father is called the "Father of lights," the Son is called "the Word" and the Holy Ghost is called the "Lord and Giver of Life") and yet comprising one God. In the Western Churches, we confess that the Holy Ghost proceeds from the Father and the Son.

NOTES:

God Is the Creator

God is the Creator of the universe and is Himself uncreated and outside of time and space. He is King of kings and Lord of lords, and He has said, "Thou shalt have no other gods before me" (Exodus 20:3).

Contrary to the teachings of the heretic Gnostics, God did not create a "demiurge" who then created the flawed material world. God Himself created all that there is, both visible and invisible, including planets, stars, angels, mankind, beasts, heaven, and hell. All that is visible and invisible was created by God alone.

- **Genesis 1:** ¹In the beginning **God created the heaven and the earth.** ²And the earth was without form, and void; and darkness was upon the face of the deep. And the Spirit of God moved upon the face of the waters.
- **John 1:** ¹In the beginning was the Word, and the Word was with God, and the Word was God. ²The same was in the beginning with God. ³**All things were made by him;** and without him was not any thing made that was made.

- **Colossians 1:** [12] Giving thanks unto the Father, which hath made us meet to be partakers of the inheritance of the saints in light: [13] Who hath delivered us from the power of darkness, and hath translated us into the kingdom of his dear Son: [14] In whom we have redemption through his blood, even the forgiveness of sins: [15] Who is the image of the invisible God, the firstborn of every creature: [16] **For by him were all things created, that are in heaven, and that are in earth, visible and invisible, whether they be thrones, or dominions, or principalities, or powers: all things were created by him, and for him:** [17] And he is before all things, and by him all things consist. [18] And he is the head of the body, the church: who is the beginning, the firstborn from the dead; that in all things he might have the preeminence. [19] For it pleased the Father that in him should all fulness dwell; [20] And, having made peace through the blood of his cross, by him to reconcile all things unto himself; by him, I say, whether they be things in earth, or things in heaven.

When we confess in the **Nicene Creed** that we believe in "all things visible and invisible," we are confessing not only that God has created both the visible and invisible worlds, but also that God Himself in His fullness is invisible. Jesus declares to the Samaritan woman:

- **John 4:** [23] But the hour cometh, and now is, when the true worshippers shall worship the Father in spirit and in truth: for the Father seeketh such to worship him. [24] **God is a Spirit:** and they that worship him must worship him in spirit and in truth. [25] The woman saith unto him, I know that Messias cometh, which is called Christ: when he is come, he will tell us all things. [26] Jesus saith unto her, I that speak unto thee am he.

Summary

There is no being or entity higher—in heaven or on earth, in the universe, or in any dimension of time or space—than God Almighty. He alone is to be worshipped. To Him alone are our sacrifices of praise and thanksgiving due. God created everything, both visible and invisible. People have fallen into grievous, damnable error by worshiping the creation instead of the Creator (to learn more about this, read the first chapter of Romans).

NOTES:

NOTES:

Jesus Was Begotten, Not Created

- **John 1:** ¹In the beginning was the Word, **and the Word was with God, and the Word was God.** ²The same was in the beginning with God. ³All things were made by him; and without him was not any thing made that was made. ¹⁴And the Word was made flesh, and dwelt among us, (and we beheld his glory, the glory as of **the only begotten of the Father,**) full of grace and truth.
- **John 3:** ¹⁶For God so loved the world, that he gave his **only begotten Son,** that whosoever believeth in him should not perish, but have everlasting life.
- **Hebrews 1:** ¹God, who at sundry times and in divers manners spake in time past unto the fathers by the prophets, ²Hath in these last days spoken unto us by his Son, whom he hath appointed heir of all things, by whom also he made the worlds; ³**Who being the brightness of his glory, and the express image of his person, and**

upholding all things by the word of his power, when he had by himself purged our sins, sat down on the right hand of the Majesty on high: [4] Being made so much better than the angels, as he hath by inheritance obtained a more excellent name than they. [5] **For unto which of the angels said he at any time, Thou art my Son, this day have I begotten thee? And again, I will be to him a Father, and he shall be to me a Son?** [6] **And again, when he bringeth in the firstbegotten into the world, he saith, And let all the angels of God worship him.** [7] And of the angels he saith, Who maketh his angels spirits, and his ministers a flame of fire. [8] But unto the Son he saith, Thy throne, O God, is for ever and ever: a sceptre of righteousness is the sceptre of thy kingdom.

- In the **Nicene Creed** we confess: "I believe ... in one Lord Jesus Christ, the only-begotten Son of God; **Begotten of his Father before all worlds, God of God, Light of Light, Very God of Very God; Begotten, not made; Being of one substance with the Father;** By whom all things were made."

The Son is the second Person of the Trinity, and as such, He is fully God, and not some "lesser" version of God. The Father did not create the Son, but the Son was begotten of the Father in eternity. The Son exists co-eternally within the Godhead together with the Father and the Holy Spirit.

To set an example for mankind, and to reflect His willing subordination to God, having taken on the "likeness of men" (Philippians 2:7), Jesus prayed to God, allowed Himself to be baptized by John, and said, "the Father is greater than I" (John 14:28). Some have falsely taken this to mean that the eternally begotten Son of God is lower than the Father or not as powerful or as divine. This is a heretical teaching.

Summary

The Son of God *is* God, eternally begotten of the Father. He is one with the Father, and is not lesser than the Father. He is of "one substance" with the Father. He is worshipped and praised as God.

NOTES:

The Gospel Is Good News

Good News From the Beginning

The gospel literally means "good news" and good news it is, indeed! When God created the heavens and the earth, the angels had already been created, and the great rebellion had already taken place in heaven: The fallen angels, led by Lucifer, rebelled against God were cast out of heaven. Lucifer and those fallen angels whom we know as demons refused to serve man, the crowning jewel of God's creation. Although angels were created with free will (without which they could not have rebelled), they were in no way created in the "image and likeness of God" and therefore could never truly be one with Him. The purpose of the angels is to serve God's creation, and that includes human beings, but the motto of Lucifer is "*non serviam*" (I will not serve), and that is because of his pride, which became his eternal downfall. Because Lucifer refused to serve the "lesser" creature of man, he set out to destroy mankind out of hatred for him. The way he went about doing that was to cause him to rebel against God, because he knew that the price of such rebellion is death.

In the Garden of Eden, first Eve was tempted by Lucifer (under the guise of the serpent) to disobey, and then Adam was. Because they both sinned, our original parents fell under a curse—but with the promise of salvation attached to it, which will become clearer as this chapter unfolds.

This curse of sin and death causes us to sin, to age, to get sick, and ultimately to die.

- **Genesis 3:** ¹ Now the serpent was more subtil than any beast of the field which the LORD God had made. And he said unto the woman, Yea, hath God said, Ye shall not eat of every tree of the garden? ² And the woman said unto the serpent, We may eat of the fruit of the trees of the garden: ³ **But of the fruit of the tree which is in the midst of the garden, God hath said, Ye shall not eat of it, neither shall ye touch it, lest ye die.** ⁴ **And the serpent said unto the woman, Ye shall not surely die:** ⁵ For God doth know that in the day ye eat thereof, then your eyes shall be opened, and ye shall be as gods, knowing good and evil. ⁶ And when the woman saw that the tree was good for food, and that it was pleasant to the eyes, and a tree to be desired to make one wise, she took of the fruit thereof, and did eat, and gave also unto her husband with her; and he did eat. ⁷ And the eyes of them both were opened, and they knew that they were naked; and they sewed fig leaves together, and made themselves aprons. ⁸ And they heard the voice of the LORD God walking in the garden in the cool of the day: and Adam and his wife hid themselves from the presence of the LORD God amongst the trees of the garden.

Man Was Created to Be Both Below and Above the Angels

Ontologically speaking, man was created to be both above and below the angels simultaneously. Like the angels, Adam and Eve had free will; unlike the angels, man was made in the "image and likeness of God" and therefore shared God's nature. Man is inferior to the angels in that angels have greater power, wisdom, and ability; for instance, they can see the invisible realm (since they, as spirits, live in that realm), whereas we live in the corporeal world and are therefore more limited:

- **Hebrews 2:** ⁵ For unto the angels hath he not put in subjection the world to come, whereof we speak. ⁶ But one in a certain place testified, saying, What is man, that thou art mindful of him? or the son of man that thou visitest him? ⁷ **Thou madest him a little lower than the angels; thou crownedst him with glory and honour, and didst set him over the works of thy hands:** ⁸ Thou hast put all things in subjection under his feet. For in that he put all in subjection under him, he left nothing that is not put under him. But now we see not yet all things put under him.
- **Psalm 82:** ¹ God standeth in the congregation of the mighty; he judgeth among the gods. ... ³ Defend the poor and fatherless: do justice to the afflicted and needy. ⁴ Deliver the poor and needy: rid them out of the hand of the wicked. ⁵ They know not, neither will they understand; they walk on in darkness: all the foundations of the

> earth are out of course. ⁶ I have said, **Ye are gods; and all of you are children of the most High.** ⁷ But ye shall die like men, and fall like one of the princes. ⁸ Arise, O God, judge the earth: for thou shalt inherit all nations.

God put Adam and Eve into the Garden of Eden as stewards over His creation. They were in full communion with Him, and He gave them their heart's desire—except that He warned them not to eat of the fruit of the tree of the knowledge of good and evil:

- **Genesis 2:** ¹⁵ And the Lord God took the man, and put him into the garden of Eden to dress it and to keep it. ¹⁶ And the Lord God commanded the man, saying, Of every tree of the garden thou mayest freely eat: ¹⁷ **But of the tree of the knowledge of good and evil, thou shalt not eat of it: for in the day that thou eatest thereof thou shalt surely die.**

The Fall of Man in Eden

Every Christian knows, understands, and believes that both Adam and Eve *did* take and eat of that forbidden fruit, obeying the voice of the evil one, the enemy of all mankind, who refuses to serve and obey God and to serve man. For this reason, Adam and Eve fell under God's curse, but the promise of salvation was given to them from the beginning:

- **Genesis 3:** ⁹And the Lord God called unto Adam, and said unto him, Where art thou? ¹⁰And he said, I heard thy voice in the garden, and I was afraid, because I was naked; and I hid myself. ¹¹And he said, Who told thee that thou wast naked? Hast thou eaten of the tree, whereof I commanded thee that thou shouldest not eat? ¹²And the man said, The woman whom thou gavest to be with me, she gave me of the tree, and I did eat. ¹³And the Lord God said unto the woman, What is this that thou hast done? And the woman said, The serpent beguiled me, and I did eat. ¹⁴And the Lord God said unto the serpent, Because thou hast done this, thou art cursed above all cattle, and above every beast of the field; upon thy belly shalt thou go, and dust shalt thou eat all the days of thy life: **[Here is the gospel:]** ¹⁵**And I will put enmity**

between thee and the woman, and between thy seed and her seed; it shall bruise thy head, and thou shalt bruise his heel. [16] Unto the woman he said, I will greatly multiply thy sorrow and thy conception; in sorrow thou shalt bring forth children; and thy desire shall be to thy husband, and he shall rule over thee. [17] And unto Adam he said, Because thou hast hearkened unto the voice of thy wife, and hast eaten of the tree, of which I commanded thee, saying, Thou shalt not eat of it: cursed is the ground for thy sake; in sorrow shalt thou eat of it all the days of thy life; [18] Thorns also and thistles shall it bring forth to thee; and thou shalt eat the herb of the field; [19] In the sweat of thy face shalt thou eat bread, till thou return unto the ground; for out of it wast thou taken: for dust thou art, and unto dust shalt thou return. [20] ... [22] And the Lord God said, Behold, the man is become as one of us, to know good and evil: and now, lest he put forth his hand, and take also of the tree of life, and eat, and live for ever: [23] Therefore the Lord God sent him forth from the

> garden of Eden, to till the ground from whence he was taken. ²⁴ So he drove out the man; and he placed at the east of the garden of Eden Cherubims, and a flaming sword which turned every way, to keep the way of the tree of life.

Since through the woman Eve, all mankind came under God's curse, God saw fit for salvation to come through the woman Mary, through whom all mankind was blessed. The gospel message is somewhat cryptic in the above passage, but the promise is this: Whereas Lucifer shall only bruise the "heel" of the seed of Mary, the seed of Mary (Christ) will bruise Lucifer's "head," meaning Lucifer (including death and hell) will be utterly destroyed in the end by the promised Messiah.

Again, the "woman" in Genesis refers to the Virgin Mary, who reversed the *non serviam* of Lucifer by her *fiat*, which in her humility means, "Let it be done" (meaning she gave her assent to become the mother of the Messiah—Lucifer's "no" became Mary's "yes").[5]

---

[5] Please read, as a cross-reference for further study, *A Via Media for Anglicans on the Subject of Mary,*

- In the **Nicene Creed** we confess: "Who for us men and for our salvation came down from heaven, **And was incarnate by the Holy Ghost of the Virgin Mary, And was made man.**"
- In the *Magnificat*, also known as the Canticle of Mary, we see how Mary reverses the curse brought to mankind through the disobedience of Eve:
Luke 1: [46] And Mary said, My soul doth magnify the Lord, [47] And my spirit hath rejoiced in God my Saviour. [48] For he hath regarded the low estate of his handmaiden: **for, behold, from henceforth all generations shall call me blessed.** [49] For he that is mighty hath done to me great things; and holy is his name. [50] And his mercy is on them that fear him from generation to generation. [51] He hath shewed strength with his arm; he hath scattered the proud in the imagination of their hearts. [52] He hath put down the mighty from their seats, and exalted them of low degree. [53] He hath filled the hungry with good things; and the rich he hath

---

written by Deaconess Lisa DellaVecchia and available through The Jeremiad Christian Homesteaders Gazette and associated vendors.

sent empty away. ⁵⁴ He hath helped his servant Israel, in remembrance of his mercy; ⁵⁵ As he spake to our fathers, to Abraham, and to his seed for ever.

The Gospel Explained

- **1 Corinthians 15:** ²¹ For since by man came death, by man came also the resurrection of the dead. ²² **For as in Adam all die, even so in Christ shall all be made alive.** ²³ But every man in his own order: Christ the firstfruits; afterward they that are Christ's at his coming. ²⁴ Then cometh the end, when he shall have delivered up the kingdom to God, even the Father; when he shall have put down all rule and all authority and power. ²⁵ For he must reign, till he hath put all enemies under his feet. ²⁶ The last enemy that shall be destroyed is death.

Summary

Although each one of us is born with the stain of Original Sin inherited from Adam and Eve, and thus we are inclined to do evil and to turn away from God by nature, we have a Redeemer who has provided an escape from eternal death and hell. By His stripes we are healed. If we believe in Him, and what He did on our behalf, and if we devote our lives to loving and obeying Him, we have an "Advocate with the Father" (1 John 2:1) who argues our case before the Father and defends us through the power of His blood. By His death and resurrection—his one, perfect, and sufficient sacrifice—Jesus defeated sin, death, and hell so that we may live eternally with Him in glory. This is the good news of the gospel!

NOTES:

Sinners Need the Savior

We know that we need Jesus to get us through life and to carry us to heaven when take our last breath. We know that we cannot make it to heaven by our own effort, merit, or virtue. We sense not only our own fallen nature, but the fallen state of the entire world. It's impossible to look at the news and not see a sin-sick world drowning in evil, and we see the fruits of human wickedness: rebellion, despair, self-destruction, violence, and death.

When an infant is baptized, that infant enters the family of the Church, but the baby's family—together with the Church—is responsible for bringing that child up in the "nurture and admonition of the Lord" (Ephesians 4:16). When the child grows to the age of accountability (some say that age is about 12 years old), the child becomes personally culpable for their sins. It is at that point when confession of sins becomes a part of the Christian walk. It isn't just done once at the time of Confirmation.

What Does the Bible Say About Our Sinful State?

- **Jeremiah 17:** [9] The heart is deceitful above all things, and desperately wicked: who can know it?
- **Ecclesiastes 7:** [20] For there is not a just man upon earth, that doeth good, and sinneth not.
- **Romans 3:** [10] As it is written, There is none righteous, no, not one: [11] There is none that understandeth, there is none that seeketh after God. [12] They are all gone out of the way, they are together become unprofitable; **there is none that doeth good, no, not one.** [13] Their throat is an open sepulchre; with their tongues they have used deceit; the poison of asps is under their lips: [14] Whose mouth is full of cursing and bitterness: [15] Their feet are swift to shed blood: [16] Destruction and misery are in their ways: [17] And the way of peace have they not known: [18] There is no fear of God before their eyes.
- **1 John 1:** [7] But if we walk in the light, as he is in the light, we have fellowship one with another, and the blood of Jesus Christ his Son cleanseth

us from all sin. **⁸ If we say that we have no sin, we deceive ourselves, and the truth is not in us.** ⁹ If we confess our sins, he is faithful and just to forgive us our sins, and to cleanse us from all unrighteousness. ¹⁰ If we say that we have not sinned, we make him a liar, and his word is not in us.

Summary

The first step in becoming a believer in Christ is to acknowledge your own sinful state, to believe that your sinfulness requires punishment and results in damnation, and to repent—which means to "turn back," "turn around," or "change your mind." Your earnest desire is to be delivered from the inevitable consequence of sin without Christ: being eternally separated from God and thus destined for hell. When we are in this state of sorrow for sin, and we are desirous of deliverance, we become what is known as a *penitent*. In a sense, every catechumen is a penitent.

NOTES:

We Confess and Are Forgiven

Christians confess their sins every Sunday as part of the Liturgy, but they also should confess regularly in the silence of their hearts before the Lord, asking Him to forgive sins they have committed. While only God Himself can forgive sins, God gives the Church, through the priests and bishops, the power to invoke His forgiveness of sins through the act of *absolution*:

- **John 20:** [21] Then said Jesus to them again, Peace be unto you: as my Father hath sent me, even so send I you. [22] And when he had said this, he breathed on them, and saith unto them, Receive ye the Holy Ghost: [23] **Whose soever sins ye remit, they are remitted unto them; and whose soever sins ye retain, they are retained.**
- In the **Apostles' Creed** we confess: "I believe in ... **the forgiveness of sins**."

Whether one is baptized as an infant or baptized as an adult, the Christian life is not "once and done" or "set it and forget it": It is, rather, a daily walk with God, staying in close fellowship with Him, confessing our faults both to him and to one another. We do receive the "remission of sins" at Baptism (Nicene Creed), but confession and absolution are ongoing throughout a Christian's life.

Some important passages on sin and the need for regular confession are provided here:

- **Isaiah 59:** [1] Behold, the Lord's hand is not shortened, that it cannot save; neither his ear heavy, that it cannot hear: [2] **But your iniquities have separated between you and your God, and your sins have hid his face from you, that he will not hear.** [3] For your hands are defiled with blood, and your fingers with iniquity; your lips have spoken lies, your tongue hath muttered perverseness.
- **Matthew 3:** [1] In those days came John the Baptist, preaching in the wilderness of Judaea, [2] And saying, Repent ye: for the kingdom of heaven is at hand. [3] For this is he that was spoken of by the prophet Esaias, saying, The voice of one crying in the

wilderness, Prepare ye the way of the Lord, make his paths straight. [4] And the same John had his raiment of camel's hair, and a leathern girdle about his loins; and his meat was locusts and wild honey. [5] Then went out to him Jerusalem, and all Judaea, and all the region round about Jordan, [6] And were baptized of him in Jordan, **confessing their sins.**

- **1 John 1:** [9] If we **confess our sins,** he is faithful and just to forgive us our sins, and to cleanse us from all unrighteousness. [10] If we say that we have not sinned, we make him a liar, and his word is not in us.
- **James 5:** [16] **Confess your faults one to another,** and pray one for another, that ye may be healed. The effectual fervent prayer of a righteous man availeth much.
- **Acts 3 [Saint Peter speaking]:** [19] **Repent ye therefore, and be converted,** that your sins may be blotted out, when the times of refreshing shall come from the presence of the Lord. [20] And he shall send Jesus Christ, which before was preached unto you: [21] Whom the

heaven must receive until the times of restitution of all things, which God hath spoken by the mouth of all his holy prophets since the world began.

Summary

It is necessary not only to recognize that we are sinners, but to diligently stay in a confessional state as Christians. We must not be nonchalant about our sins or simply keep sinning because "Jesus paid it all"; rather, we must confess our sins regularly so as to receive forgiveness and stay in a right relationship with God (Isaiah 59:2). We publicly confess our sins at every Sunday Mass, but for very serious sins, Christians are also able to meet with a priest for private confession, absolution, and penance.

NOTES:

NOTES:

Jesus Is Our Redeemer

Since God cursed mankind, only God Himself could lift that curse. Only God Himself could in fact pay the price of satisfaction or atonement for the cursed state under which all of creation fell in that moment when Adam and Eve chose to rebel against God despite all of His love and goodness toward them.

However, in order for mankind to understand the depth of its own depravity, God in the interim gave mankind His Law through Moses. We know this as the Law of Moses, or the Mosaic Law. Because the Law is from God, it is pure and holy—but nobody can be saved by it. This is the key mistake that unbelieving Jews, under-catechized Christians, and heretics make. They think they can save themselves by their own righteousness. If it were true that the Law could save, then there would never have been a need for a Redeemer at all, and then this would make God a liar, since the entire Old Testament points to the Messiah, or Redeemer, who will bring Salvation to a sin-sick world.

Therefore, the Law had to serve some *other* purpose. We learn in the book of Romans that the Law was given as a schoolmaster and a curse from which Christ saved us. Why is the Law a curse? It's because if you are guilty of even one iota of the Law, you are guilty of the whole Law—even though "there is none that doeth good, no, not one" (Psalm 53:3).

- **James 2:** [10] For whosoever shall keep the whole law, and yet offend in one point, he is guilty of all.
- **Galatians 3: [10] For as many as are of the works of the law are under the curse:** for it is written, Cursed is every one that continueth not in all things which are written in the book of the law to do them. [11] But that no man is justified by the law in the sight of God, it is evident: for, The just shall live by faith. [12] And the law is not of faith: but, The man that doeth them shall live in them. [13] Christ hath redeemed us from the curse of the law, being made a curse for us: for it is written, Cursed is every one that hangeth on a tree: ... [21] Is the law then against the promises of God? God forbid: for if there had

been a law given which could have given life, verily righteousness should have been by the law. ²² But the scripture hath concluded all under sin, that the promise by faith of Jesus Christ might be given to them that believe. ²³ But before faith came, we were kept under the law, shut up unto the faith which should afterwards be revealed. ²⁴ Wherefore the law was our schoolmaster to bring us unto Christ, that we might be justified by faith. ²⁵ But after that faith is come, we are no longer under a schoolmaster. ²⁶ For ye are all the children of God by faith in Christ Jesus.²⁷ For as many of you as have been baptized into Christ have put on Christ.

God promises that His "own arm" will redeem Israel—meaning Himself and no other, since no other could do it:

- **Isaiah 63:** ⁵ And I looked, and there was none to help; and I wondered that there was none to uphold: **therefore mine own arm brought salvation** unto me; and my fury, it upheld me ...⁷ I will mention the lovingkindnesses of the Lord, and the praises of the Lord, according to all that the Lord hath bestowed on us, and the great goodness toward the house of Israel, which he hath bestowed on them according to his mercies, and according to the multitude of his lovingkindnesses. [8] For he said, Surely they are my people, children that will not lie: so he was their Saviour. [9] In all their affliction he was afflicted, and the angel of his presence saved them: in his love and in his pity he redeemed them; and he bare them, and carried them all the days of old.

- **Romans 8:** [20] For the creature was made subject to vanity, not willingly, but by reason of him who hath subjected the same in hope, [21] Because the creature itself also shall be delivered from the bondage of corruption into the glorious liberty of the children of God. [22] **For we know that the whole creation groaneth and travaileth in pain together until now.** [23] And not only they, but ourselves also, which have the firstfruits of the Spirit, even we ourselves groan within ourselves, waiting for the adoption, to wit, the redemption of our body.

Summary

Since God was the One who put all of His creation under a curse, only God could redeem creation by becoming *incarnate*, taking on human form so that He could reconcile mankind and all creation to Himself and thereby save us. It is by faith in Him that we are saved, not by our own good deeds. Although we were banished from the Garden of Eden, we will return to Paradise once again. "Behold, I make all things new," says our great Redeemer (Revelation 21:5).

NOTES:

Jesus Was Born of a Virgin

The most memorable gospel passage in the Bible is this: "For God so loved the world, that he gave his only begotten Son, that whosoever believeth in him should not perish, but have everlasting life" (John 3:16). But how did God "give" his "only begotten Son" to us, and why was it necessary for God to take on the "likeness of men" in order to procure our salvation? These are very complex theological ideas, but we can try to unpack them by taking a look at some Bible passages.

A "Prophet Like Unto Moses"

It was necessary for the Word of God to be made flesh and dwell among us (John 1) in order to save us from our sins—first and foremost, because only blood can atone for sins, and His sacrificed blood is perfect; second, because we cannot know God in his fullness and be in relationship with Him without actually dying—His majesty is simply too overwhelming for sinful flesh and blood to withstand. This is why it was prophesied in Deuteronomy that the future

Messiah would be a "prophet like unto Moses":

- **Deuteronomy 18:** [15] The LORD thy God will raise up unto thee a Prophet from the midst of thee, of thy brethren, like unto me; unto him ye shall hearken; [16] According to all that thou desiredst of the LORD thy God in Horeb in the day of the assembly, saying, **Let me not hear again the voice of the LORD my God, neither let me see this great fire any more, that I die not.** [17] And the LORD said unto me, They have well *spoken that* which they have spoken. [18] **I will raise them up a Prophet from among their brethren, like unto thee, and will put my words in his mouth; and he shall speak unto them all that I shall command him.** [19] And it shall come to pass, *that* whosoever will not hearken unto my words which he shall speak in my name, I will require *it* of him.

The words in bold above underscore why a Meditator is necessary between God and mankind: Again, human beings cannot see the fullness of God and survive. It is impossible. God in his fulness is too overwhelmingly powerful! Therefore, for God to be able to dialogue with man, let alone commune with him and save him, mankind needed a Mediator. Moses was the mediator between God and Israel; Jesus was and is the Mediator between God and all mankind. "For there is one God, and one mediator between God and men, the man Christ Jesus" (1 Timothy 3:5).

The Incarnation

That role of mediator was filled imperfectly by Moses, but "in the fullness of time" (Galatians 4:4) the Mediator was God Himself, who became incarnate by the Holy Ghost of the Virgin Mary, and was named Jesus:

- In the **Nicene Creed** we confess: Who for us men and for our salvation came down from heaven, **And was incarnate by the Holy Ghost of the Virgin Mary, And was made man.**
- **Isaiah 7:** [10] Moreover the Lord spake again unto Ahaz, saying, [11] Ask thee a sign of the Lord thy God; ask it either in the depth, or in the height above. [12] But Ahaz said, I will not ask, neither will I tempt the Lord. [13] And he said,

Hear ye now, O house of David; Is it a small thing for you to weary men, but will ye weary my God also? [14] Therefore the Lord himself shall give you a sign; **Behold, a virgin shall conceive, and bear a son,** and shall call his name Immanuel.

- **Isaiah 9:** [6] For unto us **a child is born,** unto us a son is given: and the government shall be upon his shoulder: and **his name shall be called Wonderful, Counsellor, The mighty God, The everlasting Father, The Prince of Peace.** [7] Of the increase of his government and peace there shall be no end, upon the throne of David, and upon his kingdom, to order it, and to establish it with judgment and with justice from henceforth even for ever. The zeal of the Lord of hosts will perform this.
- **Luke 1:** [26] And in the sixth month the angel Gabriel was sent from God unto a city of Galilee, named Nazareth, [27] To a virgin espoused to a man whose name was Joseph, of the house of David; and the virgin's name was Mary. [28] And the angel came in unto her, and said, Hail, thou that art highly

favoured, the Lord is with thee: blessed art thou among women. [29] And when she saw him, she was troubled at his saying, and cast in her mind what manner of salutation this should be. [30] And the angel said unto her, Fear not, Mary: for thou hast found favour with God. [31] And, behold, thou shalt conceive in thy womb, and bring forth a son, and shalt call his name JESUS. [32] He shall be great, and shall be called the Son of the Highest: and the Lord God shall give unto him the throne of his father David: [33] And he shall reign over the house of Jacob for ever; and of his kingdom there shall be no end. [34] Then said Mary unto the angel, How shall this be, seeing I know not a man? [35] And the angel answered and said unto her, **The Holy Ghost shall come upon thee, and the power of the Highest shall overshadow thee: therefore also that holy thing which shall be born of thee shall be called the Son of God.**

- **Colossians 1:** [15] **[Christ] is the image of the invisible God,** the firstborn of every creature: [16] For by him were all things created, that are in heaven, and that are in earth, visible and invisible, whether they be thrones, or dominions, or principalities, or powers: all things were created by him, and for him: [17] And he is before all things, and by him all things consist.

- **Hebrews 2:** [9] But we see Jesus, who was made a little lower than the angels for the suffering of death, crowned with glory and honour; that he by the grace of God should taste death for every man. [10] ... [14] **Forasmuch then as the children are partakers of flesh and blood, he also himself likewise took part of the same;** that through death he might destroy him that had the power of death, that is, the devil; [15] And deliver them who through fear of death were all their lifetime subject to bondage. [16] For verily he took not on him the nature of angels; but he took on him the seed of Abraham. [17] Wherefore in all things **it behoved him to be made like unto his brethren,** that he might be a merciful and faithful high priest in things pertaining to God, to make reconciliation for the sins of the people.

- **Galatians 4:** ⁴But when the fulness of the time was come, **God sent forth his son, made of a woman,** made under the law, ⁵ To redeem them that were under the law, that we might receive the adoption of sons. ⁶ And because ye are sons, God hath sent forth the Spirit of his son into your hearts, crying, Abba, Father.

Summary

It was necessary for the Son of God to take on the likeness of men, thus becoming both fully God and fully man. In doing so, He partook in our sufferings, our temptations (though being without sin), and our death, defeating Satan and hell by the substitution of Himself for us, taking the punishment that we ourselves deserve, and uniting all who will believe in Him to Himself. Without the incarnation and the sacrifice of the Son, the Lamb of God, there is no salvation and no eternal life. The incarnation of the Son of God—conceived by the power of the Holy Spirit and born of the Virgin Mary—is a core belief of Christianity. Any teaching that deviates from that core belief, in any way, is heresy.

NOTES:

Jesus Is Both Fully God and Fully Man

The true nature of Jesus Christ is not debatable for Christians: He is completely and totally God and yet also completely and totally man. If we believe He is fully man but not God (or not fully God), we negate His perfect and sufficient sacrifice as God—for only God Himself is able to remove the curse He placed on all of creation, as we have established.

If we believe that Christ is fully God but not man (or not fully man), then we negate the importance of His incarnation and the necessity of His partaking in our nature in order to redeem mankind. He experienced our temptations and weaknesses and even "became sin" for us, and yet He was without sin. "For he hath made him to be sin for us, who knew no sin; that we might be made the righteousness of God in him" (2 Corinthians 5:21).

These are truly complex topics that theologians have been debating for over 2,000 years. There is no way to capture here all of the theological arguments behind the Christian position, let alone all of the heresies that have sprouted up in rebellion against that position, but it is important for all Christians to accept the received decision of the Church: again, that Jesus Christ is—by a mystery—both fully God and fully man, united in one person, with no diminishment of either his Godhood or his manhood by this union. This concept is known as the *hypostatic union.* The orthodoxy of this concept was established indelibly for the Church in the Council of Chalcedon in 451 A.D. and must be believed by all Christians.

Jesus Is the Son of God

- **Matthew 16:** ¹⁵ He saith unto them, But whom say ye that I am? ¹⁶ And Simon Peter answered and said, **Thou art the Christ, the Son of the living God.** ¹⁷ And Jesus answered and said unto him, Blessed art thou, Simon Barjona: for flesh and blood hath not revealed it unto thee, but my Father which is in heaven.
- **John 20:** ²⁶ And after eight days again his disciples were within, and Thomas with them: then came Jesus, the doors

being shut, and stood in the midst, and said, Peace be unto you. ²⁷ Then saith he to Thomas, Reach hither thy finger, and behold my hands; and reach hither thy hand, and thrust it into my side: and be not faithless, but believing. ²⁸ **And Thomas answered and said unto him, My Lord and my God.** ²⁹ Jesus saith unto him, Thomas, because thou hast seen me, thou hast believed: blessed are they that have not seen, and yet have believed. ³⁰ And many other signs truly did Jesus in the presence of his disciples, which are not written in this book: ³¹ But these are written, that ye might believe that Jesus is the Christ, the Son of God; and that believing ye might have life through his name.

Jesus Is the Son of Man

- **Matthew 9:** ³ And, behold, certain of the scribes said within themselves, This man blasphemeth. ⁴ And Jesus knowing their thoughts said, Wherefore think ye evil in your hearts? ⁵ For whether is easier, to say, Thy sins be forgiven thee; or to say, Arise, and walk? ⁶But that ye may know that the **Son of man** hath power on earth to forgive sins, (then saith he to the sick of the palsy,) Arise, take up thy bed, and go unto thine house.

- **John 5:** ²⁵Verily, verily, I say unto you, The hour is coming, and now is, when the dead shall hear the voice of the Son of God: and they that hear shall live. ²⁶For as the Father hath life in himself; so hath he given to the Son to have life in himself; ²⁷And hath given him authority to execute judgment also, because he is the **Son of man.** ²⁸Marvel not at this: for the hour is coming, in the which all that are in the graves shall hear his voice, ²⁹And shall come forth; they that have done good, unto the resurrection of life; and they that have done evil, unto the resurrection of damnation.

Summary

Neither Christ's full divinity nor His full humanity can be disputed in any way without falling into heresy. He is fully God and fully man in a mystery called the hypostatic union. These two natures are united in one person and not mixed. They are united "without change, without division, without separation" (Council of Chalcedon, 451 A.D.) with each nature having its own unique attributes but belonging to a single person, who is Christ.

NOTES:

We Are Saved by His Redemption

You have probably heard the expression "Jesus paid it all!" He did "pay it all," but what does that even mean? The idea that someone close to us can pay the debt we owe on our behalf—debt we cannot pay—really shouldn't be foreign to us: We all know that when someone is incarcerated and bail is set, it's usually a family member who posts bail for the individual, thus freeing them from prison. This is the same idea as the "kinsman-redeemer" (in Hebrew the role is called *go'el*). Among the main responsibilities of the *go'el* was to redeem a relative from the bondage of slavery.

By taking the role of our Kinsman-Redeemer, Jesus accomplishes the following:

He Makes Us Part of His Family

We can take part in the redemption offered by our Kinsman-Redeemer by becoming part of His family. We gain entrance into the family of believers either as an adult through Baptism and Confirmation of our own accord, or by proxy through our

Christian family through infant Baptism and later through Confirmation when we are older.

- **1 John 3:** [1] **Behold, what manner of love the Father hath bestowed upon us, that we should be called the sons of God:** therefore the world knoweth us not, because it knew him not. [2] Beloved, now are we the sons of God, and it doth not yet appear what we shall be: but we know that, when he shall appear, we shall be like him; for we shall see him as he is.
- **Galatians 4:** [4] But when the fulness of the time was come, God sent forth his Son, made of a woman, made under the law, [5] To redeem them that were under the law, **that we might receive the adoption of sons.**

He Redeems Us From the Bondage of Sin:

- **John 8:** [31] Then said Jesus to those Jews which believed on him, If ye continue in my word, then are ye my disciples indeed; [32] And ye shall know the truth, and the truth shall make you free. ³³ They answered him, We be Abraham's seed, and were never in bondage to any man: how sayest thou, Ye shall be made free? ³⁴ Jesus answered them, **Verily, verily, I say unto you, Whosoever committeth sin is the servant of sin.** ³⁵ And the servant abideth not in the house for ever: but the Son abideth ever. ³⁶ If the Son therefore shall make you free, ye shall be free indeed.

- **Romans 6:** ¹⁶ Know ye not, that to whom ye yield yourselves servants to obey, his servants ye are to whom ye obey; whether of sin unto death, or of obedience unto righteousness? ¹⁷ But God be thanked, **that ye were the servants of sin,** but ye have obeyed from the heart that form of doctrine which was delivered you. ¹⁸ Being then made free from sin, ye became the servants of righteousness... ²⁰ For when ye were the servants of sin, ye were free from righteousness. ²¹ What fruit had ye then in those things whereof ye are now ashamed? for the end of those things is death. ²² But now being made free from sin, and become servants to God, ye have your fruit unto holiness, and the end everlasting life. ²³ For the wages of sin is death; but the gift of God is eternal life through Jesus Christ our Lord.

He Takes Onto Himself the Punishment We Deserve:

- **Isaiah 51:** ¹³ He is despised and rejected of men; a man of sorrows, and acquainted with grief: and we hid as it were our faces from him; he was despised, and we esteemed him not. ⁴ Surely he hath borne our griefs, and carried our sorrows: yet we did esteem him stricken, smitten of God, and afflicted. ⁵ **But he was wounded for our transgressions, he was bruised for our iniquities:** the chastisement of our peace was upon him; and with his stripes we are healed.
- **1 Peter 2:** ²¹ For even hereunto were ye called: because Christ also suffered for us, leaving us an example, that ye should follow his steps: ²² Who did no sin, neither was guile found in his mouth: ²³ Who, when he was reviled, reviled not again; when he suffered, he threatened not; but committed himself

to him that judgeth righteously: [24] **Who his own self bare our sins in his own body on the tree,** that we, being dead to sins, should live unto righteousness: by whose stripes ye were healed.

Summary

We all deserve death and hell for our wickedness: that is, our natural propensity to commit sin and rebel against God (this is known as *concupiscence*). Jesus redeemed us—reconciling us to God by becoming kin to us—from the punishment we deserve. He took our punishment onto Himself: betrayed, mocked, scourged, and ultimately crucified in a humiliating method reserved for criminals. If we believe in Him with our whole hearts and seek to do His will through obedience, we shall be saved.

NOTES:

His Sacrifice Is Perfect and Sufficient

Under the Old Covenant, Israel sacrificed clean animals as a way of ceremonially atoning for their sins, but those sacrifices could never be *sufficient*: they had to be repeated every year during the Yom Kippur festival, and the atonement could never go as deep at the atonement of the heart—but only to the purifying of the flesh.

At Yom Kippur, one goat was slain, and the blood was given as an atonement for the people; the other goat was made the scapegoat, made to go into exile into the wilderness on Israel's behalf. In both cases, the goats took upon themselves the punishment that Israel rightly deserved.

The purpose of blood as the only means of atonement is that the life (which comes from the Holy Spirit Himself, who is the Lord and Giver of Life) is in the blood, as we read:

- **Leviticus 17:** [11] For the life of the flesh is in the blood: and I have given it to you upon the altar to make an atonement for your souls: **for it is the**

blood that maketh an atonement for the soul.

Only blood can make atonement for the soul, but the blood of animals is imperfect and could only be seen as a shadow of the perfect and once-and-for-all sacrifice of Christ Himself.

- **Hebrews 9:** [6] Now when these things were thus ordained, the priests went always into the first tabernacle, accomplishing the service of God. [7] But into the second went the high priest alone once every year, not without blood, which he offered for himself, and for the errors of the people: [8] The Holy Ghost this signifying, that the way into the holiest of all was not yet made manifest, while as the first tabernacle was yet standing: [9] Which was a figure for the time then present, in which were offered both gifts and sacrifices, that could not make him that did the service perfect, as pertaining to the conscience; [10] Which stood only in meats and drinks, and divers washings, and carnal ordinances, imposed on them until the time of reformation. [11] **But Christ**

being come an high priest of good things to come, by a greater and more perfect tabernacle, not made with hands, that is to say, not of this building; ¹²**Neither by the blood of goats and calves, but by his own blood he entered in once into the holy place, having obtained eternal redemption for us.** ¹³For if the blood of bulls and of goats, and the ashes of an heifer sprinkling the unclean, sanctifieth to the purifying of the flesh: ¹⁴How much more shall the blood of Christ, who through the eternal Spirit offered himself without spot to God, purge your conscience from dead works to serve the living God?

Summary

Only the sinless blood of the Lamb saves us. The blood of animals was only a foreshadowing: the sacrifice of Christ is perfect, purifying the heart, soul, mind, and spirit and reconciling us to God.

NOTES:

We Must Observe Holy Week

Holy Week spans from Palm Sunday to Easter Sunday, with several Masses celebrated in between, as follows:

- **Palm Sunday:** Holy Week begins with Jesus's triumphant entrance into Jerusalem on Palm Sunday (also known as Passion Sunday), when the crowds waved palm branches and shouted, "Hosanna to the son of David: Blessed is he that cometh in the name of the Lord; Hosanna in the highest" (Matthew 21:9). This event occurs on the Sunday immediately before Easter.
- **Spy Wednesday:** A few days after Palm Sunday is Spy Wednesday, the day that Judas betrayed Jesus by turning Him over to His enemies in exchange for thirty pieces of silver. We certainly do not celebrate this day, but we observe it because it represents a significant turning point in the Passion story and serves as a reminder of the agony of Christ's betrayal by Judas Iscariot.

- **Maundy Thursday.** The very next day is Maundy Thursday, the day when Christ instituted the Sacrament of Holy Communion (otherwise known as the Eucharist), in which we partake in the Body and Blood of Christ, through the bread and wine—something all Christians are **commanded** to do in remembrance of His death and passion. The word "Maundy" comes from the Latin *mandatum*, which means "command" Maundy Thursday is also widely accepted as commemorating the establishment of the Priesthood, and hence the establishment of the Sacrament of Ordination (or Holy Orders). It is during Maundy Thursday that we perform the Washing of the Feet ceremony in honor of Christ's example of humility (John 13).; everything observed on Maundy Thursday is done out of obedience to Christ's commands, and all of these observances form the foundation for our Sunday worship.

- **Good Friday:** Next comes Good Friday, the day when Christ was crucified for our sins. The crucifixion occurred during Passover, further reinforcing that He is, as declared by John the Baptist, "the Lamb of God who takes away the sins of the world" (John 1:29). On Good Friday, many churches hold a *Tenebrae* service, in which the lights in the church are dimmed and then shut out completely, and the altar in the church is stripped, to reflect the darkness that fell over the earth when Jesus died. "And it was about the sixth hour, and there was a darkness over all the earth until the ninth hour. And the sun was darkened, and the veil of the temple was rent in the midst" (Luke 23:44-45). On Good Friday, Christians fast and pray, and the whole Church Universal sits in mourning.
- **Holy Saturday:** The vigil of Good Friday extends into Holy Saturday, when Christians throughout the world sit in mourning, contemplating the torture and death of the Prince of Peace. The Church unites herself to the Apostles and Disciples who walked with Him—saints who at this point

were in hiding, not fully comprehending the meaning of what happened to their Messiah, and initially in fear for their lives over the persecutions waiting for them as followers of Christ. After the Resurrection, however, all of these saints became mighty in their faith, and almost every single one ended up becoming a willing martyr for Christ.
- **Easter Sunday:** Finally, not earlier than midnight of Saturday going into Sunday, the whole Church explodes with utter joy as we celebrate the Resurrection of our Lord and Savior. The fasts are broken, and there is feasting, and singing, and jubilation! Sin, death, and hell are conquered forever! Easter is the holiest of all days in the Church calendar, with Christmas being a very close second.

Belief in each of these events is vital to the faith of every Christian. We cannot be a Christian and deny that Jesus was crucified for our sins—or be ashamed of the cross in any way.

- **Galatians 6:** ¹⁴ But God forbid that I should glory, **save in the cross of our Lord Jesus Christ,** by whom the world is crucified unto me, and I unto the world.

We cannot be a Christian and declare that somehow Jesus did not actually die but rather escaped death, or only spiritually died (arguing that God cannot die, or making some other heretical claim).

- In the **Nicene Creed** we confess that He was "crucified also for us under Pontius Pilate; He suffered and was buried: And the third day he rose again according to the Scriptures."

We cannot be a Christian if we deny that in the period during which Jesus was buried in the tomb, He did not visit the souls in "prison" (translated as "hell" in the Apostle's Creed and the Athanasian Creed) to proclaim the gospel to the poor souls.

- In the **Apostles' Creed** we confess that He was "crucified, dead, and buried: He descended into hell."
- **1 Peter 3:** ¹⁸ For Christ also hath once suffered for sins, the just for the unjust, that he might bring us to God,

being put to death in the flesh, but quickened by the Spirit: [19] **By which also he went and preached unto the spirits in prison;** [20] Which sometime were disobedient, when once the longsuffering of God waited in the days of Noah, while the ark was a preparing, wherein few, that is, eight souls were saved by water. [21] The like figure whereunto even baptism doth also now save us (not the putting away of the filth of the flesh, but the answer of a good conscience toward God,) by the resurrection of Jesus Christ: [22] Who is gone into heaven, and is on the right hand of God; angels and authorities and powers being made subject unto him.

And finally, we cannot be a Christian if we deny the Resurrection of Christ as well as the resurrection of our *own* bodies. If we deny the resurrection, we deny that Jesus defeated death and hell on our behalf, and we are hopelessly lost in self-deception and are most to be pitied in all the earth, as the Apostle Paul wrote:

- **1 Corinthians 15:** [12] Now if Christ be preached that he rose from the dead, how say some among you that there is no resurrection of the dead? [13] But if there be no resurrection of the dead, then is Christ not risen: [14] And if Christ be not risen, then is our preaching vain, and your faith is also vain. [15] Yea, and we are found false witnesses of God; because we have testified of God that he raised up Christ: whom he raised not up, if so be that the dead rise not. [16] For if the dead rise not, then is not Christ raised: [17] And if Christ be not raised, your faith is vain; ye are yet in your sins. [18] Then they also which are fallen asleep in Christ are perished. [19] **If in this life only we have hope in Christ, we are of all men most miserable.** [20] But now is Christ risen from the dead, and become the firstfruits of them that slept. [21] For since by man came death, by man came also the resurrection of the dead. [22] For as in Adam all die, even so in Christ shall all be made alive.
- **1 Corinthians 15:** [51] Behold, I shew you a mystery; We shall not all sleep, but we shall all be changed, [52] In a moment,

in the twinkling of an eye, at the last trump: for the trumpet shall sound, **and the dead shall be raised incorruptible, and we shall be changed.** [53] For this corruptible must put on incorruption, and this mortal must put on immortality. [54] So when this corruptible shall have put on incorruption, and this mortal shall have put on immortality, then shall be brought to pass the saying that is written, Death is swallowed up in victory. [55] **O death, where is thy sting? O grave, where is thy victory?** [56] **The sting of death is sin; and the strength of sin is the law.** [57] **But thanks be to God, which giveth us the victory through our Lord Jesus Christ.**

- **Job 19:** [25] For I know that my redeemer liveth, and that he shall stand at the latter day upon the earth: [26] And though after my skin worms destroy this body, yet in my flesh shall I see God: [27] Whom I shall see for myself, and mine eyes shall behold, and not another; though my reins be consumed within me.

- In the **Nicene Creed** we confess: "I look for **the Resurrection of the dead**: And the Life of the world to come. Amen."

Summary

Holy Week is the holiest period of the Church calendar. It immediately follows the 40-day fasting season of Lent, and it commemorates the passion, death, burial, and resurrection of Our Lord. As Christians, we walk with Christ during this entire period, which starts with fasting and repentance and ends with a glorious celebration of the Resurrection. Each year, we follow the Liturgical Calendar and repeat these spiritual exercises in unity with one another, as one Body of Christ through the Church. Although different Christian faith traditions may celebrate these holidays in different ways, the spirit and intent are the same throughout all of mainstream Christianity.

NOTES:

He Ascended and Will Return Again

After Jesus's resurrection from the dead, which occurred Easter Sunday, Jesus appeared to his disciples and many others. For forty days He stayed among His followers and comforted them, but then it came time to depart, as we read the account of the Ascension:

- **Acts 1:** ¹ The former treatise have I made, O Theophilus, of all that Jesus began both to do and teach, ² Until the day in which he was taken up, after that he through the Holy Ghost had given commandments unto the apostles whom he had chosen: ³ To whom also he shewed himself alive after his passion by many infallible proofs, being seen of them forty days, and speaking of the things pertaining to the kingdom of God: ⁴ And, being assembled together with them, commanded them that they should not depart from Jerusalem, but wait for the promise of the Father, which, saith he, ye have heard of me. ⁵ For John truly baptized with water; but ye shall be baptized with the Holy Ghost not many days hence. ⁶ When they therefore were come together, they asked of him, saying, Lord, wilt thou at this time restore again the kingdom to Israel? ⁷ And he said unto them, It is not for you to know the times or the seasons, which the Father hath put in his own power. ⁸ But ye shall receive power, after that the Holy Ghost is come upon you: and ye shall be witnesses unto me both in Jerusalem, and in all Judaea, and in Samaria, and unto the uttermost part of the earth. ⁹ **And when he had spoken these things, while they beheld, he was taken up; and a cloud received him out of their sight.** ¹⁰ And while they looked stedfastly toward heaven as he went up, behold, two men stood by them in white apparel; ¹¹ Which also said, Ye men of Galilee, why stand ye gazing up into heaven? **this same Jesus, which is taken up from you into heaven, shall so come in like manner as ye have seen him go into heaven.**

- **Mark 14:** ⁶⁰ And the high priest stood up in the midst, and asked Jesus, saying, Answerest thou nothing? what is it which these witness against thee? ⁶¹ But he held his peace, and answered nothing. Again the high priest asked him, and said unto him, Art thou the Christ, the Son of the Blessed? ⁶² And Jesus said, I am: **and ye shall see the Son of man sitting on the right hand of power, and coming in the clouds of heaven.**

- In the **Nicene Creed** we confess: He "ascended into heaven, And sitteth on the right hand of the Father: **and he shall come again, with glory, to judge both the quick and the dead;** Whose Kingdom shall have no end.

Summary

When Jesus first appeared to mankind, He came in the role of the Suffering Servant (Isaiah 51). When He comes again at the Second Coming, He will return as a general with an army. He will annihilate the wicked and set up His kingdom on earth (Revelation 19-20).

NOTES:

The Holy Spirit Indwells Us

Fifty days after the Resurrection of Christ, a great event happened in the life of the Church. The Holy Spirit descended upon the apostles and other disciples, in the form of tongues of fire, and from that event the Church was born!

In a wonderful reversal of the curse of the Tower of Babel, in which God cursed the people by confusing everyone's language and scattering mankind to the ends of the earth, at Pentecost, each person was able to hear the gospel in his own language! It was the power of the Holy Spirit that allowed the Apostles the ability to reach people with the truth spoken in a language they could understand. In this way, the gospel spread throughout all of Judea and beyond to the Gentile nations surrounding Judea and then much further abroad—from the Celtic lands to as far as India and even beyond.

The great miracle of Pentecost is described in the book of Acts:

- **Acts 2:** ¹And when the day of Pentecost was fully come, they were all with one accord in one place. ²And suddenly there came a sound from heaven as of a rushing mighty wind, and it filled all the house where they were sitting. ³ **And there appeared unto them cloven tongues like as of fire, and it sat upon each of them. ⁴ And they were all filled with the Holy Ghost, and began to speak with other tongues,** as the Spirit gave them utterance. ⁵ And there were dwelling at Jerusalem Jews, devout men, out of every nation under heaven. ⁶ Now when this was noised abroad, the multitude came together, and were confounded, because that every man heard them speak in his own language. ⁷ And they were all amazed and marvelled, saying one to another, Behold, are not all these which speak Galilaeans? ⁸ And how hear we every man in our own tongue, wherein we were born? ⁹ Parthians, and Medes, and Elamites, and the dwellers in Mesopotamia, and in Judaea, and Cappadocia, in Pontus, and Asia, ¹⁰ Phrygia, and Pamphylia, in Egypt, and in the parts of Libya about Cyrene, and strangers of Rome, Jews and proselytes, ¹¹ Cretes and Arabians, we do hear them speak in our tongues the wonderful works of God. ¹² And they were all amazed, and were in doubt, saying one to another, What meaneth this? ¹³ Others mocking said, These men are full of new wine. ¹⁴ But Peter, standing up with the eleven, lifted up his voice, and said unto them, Ye men of Judaea, and all ye that dwell at Jerusalem, be this known unto you, and hearken to my words: ¹⁵ For these are not drunken, as ye suppose, seeing it is but the third hour of the day. ¹⁶ But this is that which was spoken by the prophet Joel; ¹⁷ And it shall come to pass in the last days, saith God, I will pour out of my Spirit upon all flesh: and your sons and your daughters shall prophesy, and your young men shall see visions, and your old men shall dream dreams: ¹⁸ And on my servants and on my handmaidens I will pour out in those days of my Spirit; and they shall prophesy: ¹⁹ And I will shew wonders in heaven above, and signs in the earth beneath; blood, and fire, and vapour of smoke: ²⁰ The sun shall be turned into darkness, and the moon into blood, before the great and notable day of the Lord come: ²¹

And it shall come to pass, that whosoever shall call on the name of the Lord shall be saved. [22] Ye men of Israel, hear these words; Jesus of Nazareth, a man approved of God among you by miracles and wonders and signs, which God did by him in the midst of you, as ye yourselves also know: [23] Him, being delivered by the determinate counsel and foreknowledge of God, ye have taken, and by wicked hands have crucified and slain: [24] Whom God hath raised up, having loosed the pains of death: because it was not possible that he should be holden of it. [25] For David speaketh concerning him, I foresaw the Lord always before my face, for he is on my right hand, that I should not be moved: [26] Therefore did my heart rejoice, and my tongue was glad; moreover also my flesh shall rest in hope: [27] Because thou wilt not leave my soul in hell, neither wilt thou suffer thine Holy One to see corruption. [28] Thou hast made known to me the ways of life; thou shalt make me full of joy with thy countenance. [29] Men and brethren, let me freely speak unto you of the patriarch David, that he is both dead and buried, and his sepulchre is with us unto this day. ³⁰ Therefore being a prophet, and knowing that God had sworn with an oath to him, that of the fruit of his loins, according to the flesh, he would raise up Christ to sit on his throne; ³¹ He seeing this before spake of the resurrection of Christ, that his soul was not left in hell, neither his flesh did see corruption. ³² This Jesus hath God raised up, whereof we all are witnesses. ³³ Therefore being by the right hand of God exalted, and having received of the Father the promise of the Holy Ghost, he hath shed forth this, which ye now see and hear. ³⁴ For David is not ascended into the heavens: but he saith himself, The Lord said unto my Lord, Sit thou on my right hand, ³⁵ Until I make thy foes thy footstool. ³⁶ Therefore let all the house of Israel know assuredly, that God hath made the same Jesus, whom ye have crucified, both Lord and Christ. ³⁷ Now when they heard this, they were pricked in their heart, and said unto Peter and to the rest of the apostles, Men and brethren, what shall

> we do?³⁸ Then Peter said unto them, **Repent, and be baptized every one of you in the name of Jesus Christ for the remission of sins, and ye shall receive the gift of the Holy Ghost.** ³⁹ For the promise is unto you, and to your children, and to all that are afar off, even as many as the Lord our God shall call. ⁴⁰ And with many other words did he testify and exhort, saying, Save yourselves from this untoward generation. ⁴¹ **Then they that gladly received his word were baptized:** and the same day there were added unto them about three thousand souls.

As you can see from the parts in bold above, Pentecost represents not only the spreading of the gospel throughout the world (also known as evangelization) but also the "gift of the Holy Ghost" through Baptism.

In the Sacrament of Baptism, each Christian receives the indwelling of the Holy Ghost. The Holy Ghost residing within us thereafter predisposes us to live in holiness, gives us discernment to "test the spirits" to know the difference between true and false teaching, inclines our hearts to humility and obedience to God, gives us courage, and inspires us to do all manner of good works.

Summary

Is it possible for someone be saved without Baptism? God can do anything, so yes, He could save someone who fully *intended* to be baptized but died beforehand. But no Christian can deny that Baptism saves (1 Peter 3:21), and they should never willingly delay taking this Sacrament, thereby shunning the grace that comes from Baptism through the Holy Spirit.

Infant baptism aside, the proper intention of a person who is starting on a journey to become a Christian is to *want* to be baptized as soon as possible. Baptism follows instruction in the fundamentals of the Christian faith and a profession of faith in Christ.

NOTES:

We Must Be Born Again

Jesus made it clear, by the analogy of only putting new wine into new wine bottles (Mark 2:22), that we must be born again into new life in Him—that through His death we must pass from death into life, walking in the Spirit:

- **John 3:** ¹ There was a man of the Pharisees, named Nicodemus, a ruler of the Jews: ² The same came to Jesus by night, and said unto him, Rabbi, we know that thou art a teacher come from God: for no man can do these miracles that thou doest, except God be with him. ³ **Jesus answered and said unto him, Verily, verily, I say unto thee, Except a man be born again, he cannot see the kingdom of God.** ⁴ Nicodemus saith unto him, How can a man be born when he is old? can he enter the second time into his mother's womb, and be born? ⁵ Jesus answered, Verily, verily, I say unto thee, **Except a man be born of water and of the Spirit, he cannot enter into the kingdom of God.**

Being born "of water and of the Spirit" is referring to Christian Baptism. We must be baptized in order to "receive the gift of the Holy Ghost" (Acts 2:38).

In the book of Matthew, John the Baptist teaches us that the Messiah baptizes us "with the Holy Ghost, and with fire"; this is a reference to that future first Pentecost in the book of Acts, when the Church received the "gift of the Holy Ghost," Who appeared to the brethren in the form of a mighty wind and tongues of fire:

- **Matthew 3:** [11] I indeed baptize you with water unto repentance. but he that cometh after me is mightier than I, whose shoes I am not worthy to bear: **he shall baptize you with the Holy Ghost, and with fire:** [12] Whose fan is in his hand, and he will throughly purge his floor, and gather his wheat into the garner; but he will burn up the chaff with unquenchable fire.

And we know that the Holy Spirit proceeds from both the Father *and* the Son, and not from the Father only (as Eastern Orthodox Christians contend).

From the Father

- **John 14:** ¹²Verily, verily, I say unto you, He that believeth on me, the works that I do shall he do also; and greater works than these shall he do; because I go unto my Father. ¹³And whatsoever ye shall ask in my name, that will I do, that the Father may be glorified in the Son. ¹⁴If ye shall ask any thing in my name, I will do it. ¹⁵If ye love me, keep my commandments. ¹⁶ **And I will pray the Father, and he shall give you another Comforter, that he may abide with you for ever;** ¹⁷ **Even the Spirit of truth;** whom the world cannot receive, because it seeth him not, neither knoweth him: but ye know him; for he dwelleth with you, and shall be in you. ¹⁸I will not leave you comfortless: I will come to you.

From the Son

- **John 20:** ²¹Then said Jesus to them again, Peace be unto you: as my Father hath sent me, even so send I you. ²² **And when he had said this, he breathed on them, and saith unto**

them, Receive ye the Holy Ghost: ²³ Whose soever sins ye remit, they are remitted unto them; and whose soever sins ye retain, they are retained.

To be born again means to be a "new man" or a new creation in Christ:

- **Ephesians 4:** ¹⁷ This I say therefore, and testify in the Lord, that ye henceforth walk not as other Gentiles walk, in the vanity of their mind, ¹⁸ Having the understanding darkened, being alienated from the life of God through the ignorance that is in them, because of the blindness of their heart: ¹⁹ Who being past feeling have given themselves over unto lasciviousness, to work all uncleanness with greediness. ²⁰ But ye have not so learned Christ; ²¹ If so be that ye have heard him, and have been taught by him, as the truth is in Jesus: ²² That ye put off concerning the former conversation the old man, which is corrupt according to the deceitful lusts; ²³ And be renewed in the spirit of your mind; ²⁴ And that ye **put on the new man, which after God is created**

in righteousness and true holiness. ²⁵ Wherefore putting away lying, speak every man truth with his neighbour: for we are members one of another. ²⁶ Be ye angry, and sin not: let not the sun go down upon your wrath: ²⁷ Neither give place to the devil. ²⁸ Let him that stole steal no more: but rather let him labour, working with his hands the thing which is good, that he may have to give to him that needeth. ²⁹ Let no corrupt communication proceed out of your mouth, but that which is good to the use of edifying, that it may minister grace unto the hearers. ³⁰ And grieve not the holy Spirit of God, whereby ye are sealed unto the day of redemption. ³¹ Let all bitterness, and wrath, and anger, and clamour, and evil speaking, be put away from you, with all malice: ³² And be ye kind one to another, tenderhearted, forgiving one another, even as God for Christ's sake hath forgiven you.

- **1 Peter 1:** ²² Seeing ye have purified your souls in obeying the truth through the Spirit unto unfeigned love of the brethren, see that ye love one another with a pure heart fervently: **²³ Being born again, not of corruptible seed, but of incorruptible, by the word of God,** which liveth and abideth for ever.

Summary

Despite the common term "born again Christian" (a tautology, really), to be born again *doesn't* mean to take on a certain evangelical flavor or to become part of only certain types of Christian denominations. Rather, every single Christian of every denomination *must* be born again! We are born again at the moment of Baptism by the power of the Holy Spirit. We continue in that regenerated life by the power of the Holy Spirit through Confirmation and through partaking in Holy Communion.

NOTES:

NOTES:

We Must Receive Sacraments

There are seven Sacraments recognized by traditional apostolic churches that span across different denominations. These seven Sacraments are:

- **Baptism**
- **Holy Communion**
- **Confirmation**
- Ordination (or Holy Orders)
- Marriage (or Holy Matrimony)
- **Reconciliation (or Confession)**
- Anointing of the Sick (or Holy Unction)

Since many of you who are studying this book are young adult *catechumens,* meaning you have not yet been baptized, but you are preparing for your Baptism, your First Communion, and your Confirmation, the first three Sacraments listed are the most important for you to learn about right now as you are studying to enter into the Church. (The Sacrament of Confession is also relevant to you and is discussed later in this catechism.) We will not address the other three Sacraments in this particular book. As you grow in your faith and Christian walk, you will learn much more and can dig as deep as you like into the other Sacraments.

Baptism

Although anyone can be baptized at any age, traditional apostolic churches generally baptize infants who are born into Christian households.

Sacred Tradition holds that infants may be baptized because when some Christians were baptized as recorded in the Bible, their entire households were baptized:

- **Acts 16:** [14] And a certain woman named Lydia, a seller of purple, of the city of Thyatira, which worshipped God, heard us: whose heart the Lord opened, that she attended unto the things which were spoken of Paul. [15] And when she was baptized, **and her household,** she besought us, saying, If ye have judged me to be faithful to the Lord, come into my house, and abide there. And she constrained us.

Moreover, we know that Christ Himself taught we should let infants and little children come to Him and not hinder them:

- **Luke 18:** ¹⁵ And they brought unto him also infants, that he would touch them: but when his disciples saw it, they rebuked them. ¹⁶ But Jesus called them unto him, and said, **Suffer little children to come unto me, and forbid them not: for of such is the kingdom of God.** ¹⁷ Verily I say unto you, Whosoever shall not receive the kingdom of God as a little child shall in no wise enter therein.

However, the Bible also gives us examples of adult converts who ask for Baptism at the moment of their internal conversion, having confessed their belief in Christ the Savior and desiring to be filled with the Holy Spirit. What better example can be given than the eunuch in the book of Acts?

- **Acts 8:** ²⁶ And the angel of the Lord spake unto Philip, saying, Arise, and go toward the south unto the way that goeth down from Jerusalem unto Gaza, which is desert. ²⁷ And he arose and went: and, behold, a man of Ethiopia, an eunuch of great authority under Candace queen of the Ethiopians, who had the charge of all her treasure, and had come to Jerusalem for to worship,

⁲⁸ Was returning, and sitting in his chariot read Esaias the prophet. ²⁹ Then the Spirit said unto Philip, Go near, and join thyself to this chariot. ³⁰ And Philip ran thither to him, and heard him read the prophet Esaias, and said, Understandest thou what thou readest? ³¹ And he said, How can I, except some man should guide me? And he desired Philip that he would come up and sit with him. ³² The place of the scripture which he read was this, He was led as a sheep to the slaughter; and like a lamb dumb before his shearer, so opened he not his mouth: ³³ In his humiliation his judgment was taken away: and who shall declare his generation? for his life is taken from the earth. ³⁴ And the eunuch answered Philip, and said, I pray thee, of whom speaketh the prophet this? of himself, or of some other man? ³⁵ Then Philip opened his mouth, and began at the same scripture, and preached unto him Jesus. ³⁶ And as they went on their way, they came unto a certain water: and the eunuch said, **See, here is water; what doth hinder me to be baptized?**

³⁷ And Philip said, If thou believest with all thine heart, thou mayest. And he answered and said, I believe that Jesus Christ is the Son of God. ³⁸ And he commanded the chariot to stand still: and they went down both into the water, both Philip and the eunuch; and he baptized him. ³⁹ And when they were come up out of the water, the Spirit of the Lord caught away Philip, that the eunuch saw him no more: and he went on his way rejoicing.

What Does the Bible Say About Baptism?

As part of the Great Commission, Jesus commands the Church to baptize souls:

- **Mark 16:** ¹⁵ And he said unto them, Go ye into all the world, and preach the gospel to every creature. ¹⁶ **He that believeth and is baptized shall be saved;** but he that believeth not shall be damned.

Baptism unites us with Christ's death and resurrection:

- **Romans 6:** ⁴Therefore **we are buried with him by baptism into death:** that like as Christ was raised up from the dead by the glory of the Father, even so we also should walk in newness of life.
- **Colossians 2:** ¹⁰And ye are complete in him, which is the head of all principality and power: ¹¹In whom also ye are circumcised with the circumcision made without hands, in putting off the body of the sins of the flesh by the circumcision of Christ: ¹² **Buried with him in baptism,** wherein also ye are risen with him through the faith of the operation of God, who hath raised him from the dead.

Baptism saves:

- **1 Peter 3:** ¹⁸For Christ also hath once suffered for sins, the just for the unjust, that he might bring us to God, being put to death in the flesh, but quickened by the Spirit: ¹⁹By which also he went and preached unto the spirits in prison; **²⁰** Which sometime were disobedient, when once the longsuffering of God waited in the days of Noah, while the ark was a preparing, wherein few, that is, eight souls were saved by water. **²¹ The like figure whereunto even baptism doth also now save us** (not the putting away of the filth of the flesh, but the answer of a good conscience toward God,) by the resurrection of Jesus Christ: **²²** Who is gone into heaven, and is on the right hand of God; angels and authorities and powers being made subject unto him.

Holy Communion

Holy Communion is, as the name suggests, an opportunity to *commune*—or unite with— Jesus Christ, our Savior. Jesus Christ instituted the Sacrament of Holy Communion during the Last Supper, which Christians commemorate during Holy Week on Maundy Thursday. During this Passover meal, Jesus gave new meaning to the elements of the Passover *seder*. Through Holy Communion, He made the teachings of the New Testament and New Covenant clear:

no longer did a lamb need to be slain and its blood painted on the doorposts year after year. The Passover story of being freed from the bondage of Egypt was but a type or a shadow of the freedom from the bondage of sin and death under which all of mankind remains without the Savior. Jesus is the true Lamb of God who takes away the sins of the world. This is the meaning of the Holy Eucharist: We partake in it to remember His death until He comes again, and we also partake in it to become one with him, so that He will strengthen us against sin, confirm us in all goodness, and bring us to everlasting life.

Christians are forbidden to partake of the Holy Eucharist if: (1) they are not baptized and confirmed; (2) they are apostate (unbelieving); (3) they are in a state of unconfessed and unabsolved sin; or (4) are not living in a state of love and charity with their neighbors. Before the giving of the Eucharist, many priest declare: "The holy things are for the holy!" This is to signal to the congregation that to be admitted to the Eucharist, the communicant must be living in a state of peace with their neighbors, not enmity; must have a clear conscience before God; and must have confessed during the

Mass and have been absolved of their sins before partaking. If the person who is approaching the altar is aware of grievous sin that is so abominable that it requires a private confession, the person must abstain from taking Communion and must reserve time with a priest so that they can make a private confession and receive absolution (and possibly penance as well).

All of this is to say that Christians cannot come to the altar to take Communion in an unprepared state; they cannot take it lightly or without faith. If they do so, they risk grave spiritual harm, for it is the Real Presence of Christ in the form of the bread and the wine that they would be consuming, and we do not want to desecrate that most holy and perfect gift.

What Does the Bible Say About Holy Communion?

Jesus commands us to partake of it, and he calls the wine His blood and the bread His body:

- **Luke 22:** ¹⁵ And he said unto them, With desire I have desired to eat this passover with you before I suffer: ¹⁶ For

I say unto you, I will not any more eat thereof, until it be fulfilled in the kingdom of God. [17] And he took the cup, and gave thanks, and said, Take this, and divide it among yourselves: [18] For I say unto you, I will not drink of the fruit of the vine, until the kingdom of God shall come. [19] And he took bread, and gave thanks, and brake it, and gave unto them, saying, **This is my body which is given for you:** this do in remembrance of me. [20] Likewise also the cup after supper, saying, **This cup is the new testament in my blood, which is shed for you.**

Jesus warns that if we refuse to partake of His body and blood, we are devoid of life:

- **John 6:** [48] I am that bread of life. [49] Your fathers did eat manna in the wilderness, and are dead. [50] This is the bread which cometh down from heaven, that a man may eat thereof, and not die. [51] I am the living bread which came down from heaven: if any man eat of this bread, he shall live for ever: and the bread that I will give is my flesh, which I will give for the life of the world. [52] The Jews therefore strove among themselves, saying, How can this man give us his flesh to eat? **⁵³ Then Jesus said unto them, Verily, verily, I say unto you, Except ye eat the flesh of the Son of man, and drink his blood, ye have no life in you. ⁵⁴ Whoso eateth my flesh, and drinketh my blood, hath eternal life; and I will raise him up at the last day. ⁵⁵ For my flesh is meat indeed, and my blood is drink indeed. ⁵⁶ He that eateth my flesh, and drinketh my blood, dwelleth in me, and I in him.** ⁵⁷ As the living Father hath sent me, and I live by the Father: so he that eateth me, even he shall live by me. ⁵⁸ This is that bread which came down from heaven: not as your fathers did eat manna, and are dead: he that eateth of this bread shall live for ever.

The Apostle Paul warns us never to take Holy Communion unworthily, because in doing so we jeopardize our salvation:

- **1 Corinthians 11:** ²³ For I have received of the Lord that which also I delivered unto you, that the Lord Jesus the same night in which he was betrayed took bread: ²⁴ And when he had given thanks, he brake it, and said, Take, eat: this is my body, which is broken for you: this do in remembrance of me. ²⁵ After the same manner also he took the cup, when he had supped, saying, this cup is the new testament in my blood: this do ye, as oft as ye drink it, in remembrance of me. ²⁶ For as often as ye eat this bread, and drink this cup, ye do shew the Lord's death till he come. ²⁷ **Wherefore whosoever shall eat this bread, and drink this cup of the Lord, unworthily, shall be guilty of the body and blood of the Lord.** ²⁸ But let a man examine himself, and so let him eat of that bread, and drink of that cup. ²⁹ For he that eateth and drinketh unworthily, eateth and drinketh damnation to himself, not discerning the Lord's body.

Confirmation

The Sacrament (or Rite) of Confirmation is not explicitly mentioned in the Bible, but it marks the passage into mature faith and full participation in the life of the Church on the part of young people. Most youngsters are confirmed at about the age of 12 or 13.

Anyone older than that age can be confirmed, but generally speaking, it does not happen at ages younger than 12. Churches presumably vary in their practices, which is perfectly fine considering that a specific age for Confirmation is not mentioned in the Bible. It just so happens, however, that the age of Confirmation generally coincides with the so-called "age of accountability" (for example, this is the age that children generally have their *bar mitzvah*). So there is a consensus that this is about the age when someone is able to become a mature participant in Church life.

Confirmands generally undergo a few years of religious instruction before they are confirmed. In the absence of such formal instruction, children are taught at home by their Christian parents.

- **Acts 8:** [14] Now when the apostles which were at Jerusalem heard that Samaria had received the word of God, they sent unto them Peter and John: [15] Who, when they were come down, **prayed for them, that they might receive the Holy Ghost:** [16] (For as yet he was fallen upon none of them: only they were baptized in the name of the Lord

Jesus.) ¹⁷ Then laid they their hands on them, and they received the Holy Ghost.
- **Acts 14:** ²¹ And when they had preached the gospel to that city, and had taught many, they returned again to Lystra, and to Iconium, and Antioch, ²² **Confirming the souls of the disciples,** and exhorting them to continue in the faith, and that we must through much tribulation enter into the kingdom of God.

Summary

The Sacraments of Baptism, Holy Communion, Confirmation, and Confession are intended for all believers. For this reason, this catechism addresses each of these Sacraments in detail.

All seven of the Holy Sacraments give the grace of the Holy Spirit in different ways, and each is vital to the Body of Christ as a whole.

The Sacrament of Ordination was first instituted by Christ at the Last Supper. This Sacrament is intended for Christian men (not women) who are called to pursue Holy

Orders (i.e., Deacon, Priest, Bishop), and they are ordained by at least one bishop in these several roles. In contrast, a deaconess is only appointed—never ordained.

The Sacrament of Marriage is only for those who are called to be married (not every Christian is called, and marriage should be prepared for and considered deeply before entering into it, as it *truly* is a Sacrament).

The Sacrament of Holy Unction is for the sick and dying: a priest or a bishop prays over and anoints the body with holy oil to heal the gravely ill, or to prepare the body and soul for a blessed death.

NOTES:

We Are Under Grace, Not the Law

Being that Christians ...

- are saved by the Blood of the Lamb
- receive the gift of the Holy Spirit at Baptism
- receive the Holy Spirit yet again at Confirmation
- are indwelled with and sealed by the Holy Spirit
- receive the most precious Body and Blood of Christ Himself
- are very members of the Body of Christ, which is the Church, of which Christ is the Head
- sons of the Father through adoption (Galatians 4:5, 1 John 3:1) ...

Christians are operating entirely in the realm of the Spirit, which is free. Christians are not under the bondage of the Law and of rules and ordinances that never saved and never *could* save, for all of these regarded the flesh and the purification of it and could never penetrate the heart.

Unless you started out in life as a religious Jew and only *later* converted to Christianity, there is no *cultural* reason for anyone to follow any of the Jewish laws and customs. And even if you are actually Jewish and later converted to Christianity, you would be in **error** if you convinced yourself (or taught anyone else) that following the Jewish laws, customs, and Sabbaths are necessary for salvation. This particular heresy is called *Judaizing,* and it is one that some early Jewish converts used to corrupt the minds of early Gentile converts. Unfortunately, this same heresy is still operative today in many quasi-Christian sects and cults.

- **Acts 15:** [5] But there rose up certain of the sect of the Pharisees which believed, saying, That it was needful to circumcise them, and to command them to keep the law of Moses. [6] And the apostles and elders came together for to consider of this matter. [7] And when there had been much disputing, Peter rose up, and said unto them, Men and brethren, ye know how that a good while ago God made choice among us, that the Gentiles by my mouth should hear the word of the gospel, and believe. [8] And God, which knoweth the hearts, bare them witness, giving them the Holy Ghost, even as he did unto us; ⁹And put no difference between us and them, purifying their hearts by faith. ¹⁰ **Now therefore why tempt ye God, to put a yoke upon the neck of the disciples, which neither our fathers nor we were able to bear?** ¹¹But we believe that through the grace of the Lord Jesus Christ we shall be saved, even as they.

- **Galatians 3:** O foolish Galatians, who hath bewitched you, that ye should not obey the truth, before whose eyes Jesus Christ hath been evidently set forth, crucified among you? ² This only would I learn of you, Received ye the Spirit by the works of the law, or by the hearing of faith? ³ **Are ye so foolish? having begun in the Spirit, are ye now made perfect by the flesh?** ⁴Have ye suffered so many things in vain? if it be yet in vain. ⁵He therefore that ministereth to you the Spirit, and worketh miracles among you, doeth he it by the works of the law, or by the hearing of faith? ⁶Even as Abraham believed God, and it was accounted to him for righteousness. ⁷Know ye therefore that they which are of faith, the same are the children of Abraham. ⁸ And the scripture, foreseeing that God would justify the heathen through faith, preached before the gospel unto Abraham, saying, In thee shall all nations be blessed. ⁹ So then they which be of faith are blessed with faithful Abraham. ¹⁰ For as many as are of the works of the law are under the curse: for it is written, Cursed is every one that continueth not in all things which are written in the book of the law to do them. **¹¹ But that no man is justified by the law in the sight of God, it is evident: for, The just shall live by faith.** ¹² **And the law is not of faith: but, The man that doeth them shall live in them.** ¹³ **Christ hath redeemed us from the curse of the law, being made a curse for us:** for it is written, Cursed is every one that hangeth on a tree: ... ²³ But before faith came, we were kept under the law, shut up unto the faith which should afterwards be revealed. ²⁴ **Wherefore the law was our schoolmaster to bring us unto Christ, that we might be justified by faith.** ²⁵ But after that faith is come,

we are no longer under a
schoolmaster.** ²⁶ For ye are all the
children of God by faith in Christ
Jesus. ²⁷ For as many of you as have
been baptized into Christ have put on
Christ.

If You Put Your Hope in the Law, You Have Fallen From Grace

- **Galatians 5:** Stand fast therefore in the liberty wherewith Christ hath made us free, and be not entangled again with the yoke of bondage. ² Behold, I Paul say unto you, that if ye be circumcised, Christ shall profit you nothing. ³ For I testify again to every man that is circumcised, that he is a debtor to do the whole law. ⁴ **Christ is become of no effect unto you, whosoever of you are justified by the law; ye are fallen from grace.**

If You Live in the Spirit, You Will Not Be Condemned

- **Romans 8:**¹ **There is therefore now no condemnation to them which are in Christ Jesus, who walk not after**

the flesh, but after the Spirit. ²For the law of the Spirit of life in Christ Jesus hath made me free from the law of sin and death. ³For what the law could not do, in that it was weak through the flesh, God sending his own Son in the likeness of sinful flesh, and for sin, condemned sin in the flesh: ⁴That the righteousness of the law might be fulfilled in us, who walk not after the flesh, but after the Spirit. ⁵For they that are after the flesh do mind the things of the flesh; but they that are after the Spirit the things of the Spirit. ⁶For to be carnally minded is death; but to be spiritually minded is life and peace. ⁷Because the carnal mind is enmity against God: for it is not subject to the law of God, neither indeed can be. ⁸So then they that are in the flesh cannot please God.

Summary

If you believe that you can only be saved by following the Law of Moses, then you are making Christ's death and sacrifice meaningless. Christ died to free Israel from the bondage of the Law, the only purpose of which was to make her aware of her state of sinfulness, bring her to a state of repentance, introduce the concept of the promised Messiah who would redeem her, and keep her ceremonially clean in the meantime—that is, until the day of the Christ's crucifixion, when the veil of the temple was torn from top to bottom and Jesus cried out with a loud voice, "It is finished." The temple in Jerusalem was destroyed in 70 A.D. Christ alone is the true Temple (John 2:19-22) and High Priest. Continuing to follow these obsolete temple laws and customs in light of Christ's death and resurrection is an insult to the salvific work of the cross of Christ. We must instead live in the Spirit under grace, in obedience to both Sacred Scripture and Sacred Tradition.

NOTES:

We Are Called to a Higher Morality

Before we go into a discussion of what morality is supposed to look like for a Christian, first we need to unpack the Mosaic Law so that we understand what pertains to us as Christians today and what does not.

The Ceremonial Law Has Been Fulfilled in Christ

The Mosaic Law consists of three parts: the *ceremonial law*, the *civil law*, and the *moral law*. In this catechism we will talk specifically about the ceremonial law versus the moral law. We can assume that the civil law given to Israel is superseded by whatever civil laws govern our conduct in our respective societies.

The ceremonial law under the Old Covenant was nailed to the cross at Christ's crucifixion; it was fulfilled the moment that Jesus declared from the cross, "It is finished" (John 19:30).

Examples of ceremonial laws are the purification laws, the sacrificial laws, the Sabbaths and new moons and festivals, rules about clean and unclean animals (*kashrut* or kosher) and other dietary practices, rules about wearing mixed clothing fibers, and many other laws designed to keep the **physical body** pure for purposes of worship in the temple.

However, there is no longer a physical temple where animal sacrifices are performed by Jewish priests—not even for the Jews who deny Christ to this day. The Church does not celebrate new moons or Sabbaths or Jewish festivals any longer. The Church does not abstain from certain meats or certain clothing types for the purification of the body. The Church comprehends that this part of the Law was fulfilled by the Lamb of God at the moment of His death:

- **John 19:** [28] After this, Jesus knowing that all things were now accomplished, that the scripture might be fulfilled, saith, I thirst. [29] Now there was set a vessel full of vinegar: and they filled a spunge with vinegar, and put it upon hyssop, and put it to his mouth. [30] When Jesus therefore had received the vinegar, he said, **It is finished:** and he bowed his head, and gave up the ghost.

- **Matthew 27:** ⁵⁰ Jesus, when he had cried again with a loud voice, yielded up the ghost. ⁵¹ And, behold, **the veil of the temple was rent in twain from the top to the bottom; and the earth did quake, and the rocks rent;** ⁵² And the graves were opened; and many bodies of the saints which slept arose, ⁵³ And came out of the graves after his resurrection, and went into the holy city, and appeared unto many. ⁵⁴ Now when the centurion, and they that were with him, watching Jesus, saw the earthquake, and those things that were done, they feared greatly, saying, Truly this was the Son of God.
- **Acts 10:** ¹⁰ And [Peter] became very hungry, and would have eaten: but while they made ready, he fell into a trance, ¹¹ And saw heaven opened, and a certain vessel descending upon him, as it had been a great sheet knit at the four corners, and let down to the earth: ¹² Wherein were all manner of fourfooted beasts of the earth, and wild beasts, and creeping things, and fowls of the air. ¹³ And there came a voice to him, Rise, Peter; kill, and eat. ¹⁴ But Peter said, Not so, Lord; for I

have never eaten any thing that is common or unclean. ¹⁵ And the voice spake unto him again the second time, **What God hath cleansed, that call not thou common.** ¹⁶ This was done thrice: and the vessel was received up again into heaven.

- **Galatians 4:** ⁴ But when the fulness of the time was come, God sent forth his Son, made of a woman, made under the law, ⁵ To redeem them that were under the law, that we might receive the adoption of sons. ⁶ And because ye are sons, God hath sent forth the Spirit of his Son into your hearts, crying, Abba, Father. ⁷ Wherefore thou art no more a servant, but a son; and if a son, then an heir of God through Christ. ⁸ Howbeit then, when ye knew not God, ye did service unto them which by nature are no gods. ⁹ But now, after that ye have known God, or rather are known of God, **how turn ye again to the weak and beggarly elements, whereunto ye desire again to be in bondage?** ¹⁰ Ye observe days, and months, and times, and years. ¹¹ I am afraid of you, lest I have bestowed upon you labour in vain.

An important admonition for Christians:

Christians influenced by the heresy of Judaizing, who observe Jewish practices (keeping kosher, observing the feast days and Sabbaths, insisting on only using Hebrew names for God, etc.)—even as a part of their own *personal and private devotion*—are putting themselves in grave spiritual danger.

Canon 8 of the Seventh Ecumenical Council (787 A.D.) rules as follows: "Since some of those who come from the religion of the Hebrews mistakenly think to make a mockery of Christ who is God, pretending to become Christians, but **denying Christ in private by both secretly continuing to observe the Sabbath and maintaining other Jewish practices,** we decree that they shall not be received to Communion or at prayer or into the church."

A Christian who follows in the footsteps of the Judaizers by adopting their Christ-rejecting practices puts themselves in a state of excommunication with the Church, even if the Church does not exercise its authority to excommunicate them.

Judaizing is condemned unequivocally by the Church. This heresy teaches that unless believers [insert some Jewish practice], they cannot be saved. Some Judaizers claiming to believe in the same Messiah that Christians believe in will even go so far as to say that all Christians are pagans, and that if Christians do not say the Sacred Name of God in Hebrew, they cannot be saved. Whatever the case, Judaizers **judge** those Christians who do not follow the ceremonial law while they themselves are pursuing heresy. Such teaching is absolutely false, harmful, and divisive, and it can have no place within the Church.

- **Ephesians 2:** [8] For **by grace** are ye saved through faith; and that not of yourselves: it is the gift of God: [9] **Not of works,** lest any man should boast.
- **Romans 14:** [5] One man esteemeth one day above another: another esteemeth every day alike. **Let every man be fully persuaded in his own mind.** [6] He that regardeth the day, regardeth it unto the Lord; and he that regardeth not the day, to the Lord he doth not regard it. He that eateth, eateth to the Lord, for he giveth God thanks; and he

that eateth not, to the Lord he eateth not, and giveth God thanks. ⁷For none of us liveth to himself, and no man dieth to himself. ⁸For whether we live, we live unto the Lord; and whether we die, we die unto the Lord: whether we live therefore, or die, we are the Lord's. ⁹For to this end Christ both died, and rose, and revived, that he might be Lord both of the dead and living. ¹⁰ **But why dost thou judge thy brother? or why dost thou set at nought thy brother? for we shall all stand before the judgment seat of Christ.** ¹¹For it is written, As I live, saith the Lord, every knee shall bow to me, and every tongue shall confess to God. ¹²So then every one of us shall give account of himself to God. ¹³Let us not therefore judge one another any more: but judge this rather, that no man put a stumblingblock or an occasion to fall in his brother's way. ¹⁴I know, and am persuaded by the Lord Jesus, **that there is nothing unclean of itself:** but to him that esteemeth any thing to be unclean, to him it is unclean.

- **Galatians 5:** ¹ Stand fast therefore in the liberty wherewith Christ hath made us free, and **be not entangled again with the yoke of bondage.** ² Behold, I Paul say unto you, that if ye be circumcised, Christ shall profit you nothing. ³ For I testify again to every man that is circumcised, that he is a debtor to do the whole law. ⁴ **Christ is become of no effect unto you, whosoever of you are justified by the law; ye are fallen from grace.** ⁵ For we through the Spirit wait for the hope of righteousness by faith. ⁶ For in Jesus Christ neither circumcision availeth any thing, nor uncircumcision; but faith which worketh by love. ⁷ Ye did run well; who did hinder you that ye should not obey the truth? ⁸ This persuasion cometh not of him that calleth you. ⁹ A little leaven leaveneth the whole lump. ¹⁰ I have confidence in you through the Lord, that ye will be none otherwise minded: but **he that troubleth you shall bear his judgment, whosoever he be.** ¹¹ And I, brethren, if I yet preach circumcision, why do I yet suffer persecution? then is the offence of the cross ceased. ¹² I would they were even cut off which trouble you. ¹³ For, brethren, ye have been called unto liberty; only use not liberty for an occasion to the flesh, but by love serve one another. ¹⁴ For all the law is fulfilled in one word, even in this; Thou shalt love thy neighbour as thyself. ¹⁵ But if ye bite and devour one another, take heed that ye be not consumed one of another. ¹⁶ This I say then, Walk in the Spirit, and ye shall not fulfil the lust of the flesh.

The Moral Law Is Still in Effect, but Christians Must Aim Even *Higher*

The moral law (in contrast to the ceremonial law), as defined in the Ten Commandments and further expounded upon in great detail in the *Torah*, is absolutely incumbent upon all Christians to follow. We know without question that we cannot worship idols, that we must honor our parents, that we must not commit adultery, or murder, or steal, or covet.

We know, too, that sexual immorality is evil (fornication, adultery, incest, homosexuality, pedophilia, bestiality, etc., as listed in both the Old and New Testaments); that idolatry, witchcraft, sorcery, necromancy, etc., are evil; that drunkenness, gluttony, riotousness, evil speech, blasphemy, etc., are evil. The list of evil thoughts and deeds could go on and on!

Nobody needs to teach us that any of these things are evil, because it is self-evident that they are. *Why?* Because the moral law is written on the human heart from the beginning of time. Even those who commit these evil deeds know that they are evil—they just do them anyway.

- **Romans 1:** [18] For the wrath of God is revealed from heaven against all ungodliness and unrighteousness of men, **who hold the truth in unrighteousness;** [19] **Because that which may be known of God is manifest in them; for God hath shewed it unto them.** [20] For the invisible things of him from the creation of the world are clearly seen, being understood by the things that are made, even his eternal power and Godhead; so that they are without excuse: [21] Because that, when they knew God, they glorified him not as

God, neither were thankful; but became vain in their imaginations, and their foolish heart was darkened. [22] Professing themselves to be wise, they became fools, [23] And changed the glory of the uncorruptible God into an image made like to corruptible man, and to birds, and fourfooted beasts, and creeping things. [24] Wherefore God also gave them up to uncleanness through the lusts of their own hearts, to dishonour their own bodies between themselves: [25] Who changed the truth of God into a lie, and worshipped and served the creature more than the Creator, who is blessed for ever. Amen. [26] For this cause God gave them up unto vile affections: for even their women did change the natural use into that which is against nature: [27] And likewise also the men, leaving the natural use of the woman, burned in their lust one toward another; men with men working that which is unseemly, and receiving in themselves that recompence of their error which was meet. [28] And even as they did not like to retain God in their knowledge, God gave them over to a reprobate mind, to do those things which are not convenient; **²⁹ Being filled with all unrighteousness, fornication, wickedness, covetousness, maliciousness; full of envy, murder, debate, deceit, malignity; whisperers, ³⁰ Backbiters, haters of God, despiteful, proud, boasters, inventors of evil things, disobedient to parents, ³¹ Without understanding, covenantbreakers, without natural affection, implacable, unmerciful: ³² Who knowing the judgment of God, that they which commit such things are worthy of death, not only do the same, but have pleasure in them that do them.**

Although every Christian knows what specific evil acts are forbidden in the *Torah*, Jesus wants us as Christians to aim even higher than simply not doing them. In Matthew 5, Jesus says we must "be perfect"; that is, we must go beyond the letter of the Law and look at the Law in a spiritual sense, after the inward man.

Jesus teaches us that we can still violate the moral law by what we are thinking and saying but not actually physically doing. In

Matthew 5, Jesus repeats "ye have heard" or "it has been said" again and again, and then challenges the believer to aim higher:

- **Matthew 5:** ¹⁹ Whosoever therefore shall break one of these least commandments, and shall teach men so, he shall be called the least in the kingdom of heaven: but whosoever shall do and teach them, the same shall be called great in the kingdom of heaven. ²⁰ For I say unto you, That except your righteousness shall exceed the righteousness of the scribes and Pharisees, ye shall in no case enter into the kingdom of heaven. ²¹ **Ye have heard that it was said of them of old time,** Thou shalt not kill; and whosoever shall kill shall be in danger of the judgment: ²² But I say unto you, That whosoever is angry with his brother without a cause shall be in danger of the judgment: and whosoever shall say to his brother, Raca, shall be in danger of the council: but whosoever shall say, Thou fool, shall be in danger of hell fire. ²³ Therefore if thou bring thy gift to the altar, and there rememberest that thy brother hath ought against thee; ²⁴ Leave there thy gift before the altar, and go thy way; first be reconciled to thy brother, and then come and offer thy gift. ²⁵ Agree with thine adversary quickly, whiles thou art in the way with him; lest at any time the adversary deliver thee to the judge, and the judge deliver thee to the officer, and thou be cast into prison. ²⁶ Verily I say unto thee, Thou shalt by no means come out thence, till thou hast paid the uttermost farthing. ²⁷ **Ye have heard that it was said by them of old time,** Thou shalt not commit adultery: ²⁸ But I say unto you, That whosoever looketh on a woman to lust after her hath committed adultery with her already in his heart. ²⁹ And if thy right eye offend thee, pluck it out, and cast it from thee: for it is profitable for thee that one of thy members should perish, and not that thy whole body should be cast into hell. ³⁰ And if thy right hand offend thee, cut it off, and cast it from thee: for it is profitable for thee that one of thy members should perish, and not that thy whole body should be cast into hell. ³¹ **It hath been**

said, Whosoever shall put away his wife, let him give her a writing of divorcement: ³²But I say unto you, That whosoever shall put away his wife, saving for the cause of fornication, causeth her to commit adultery: and whosoever shall marry her that is divorced committeth adultery. ³³Again, **ye have heard that it hath been said by them of old time**, Thou shalt not forswear thyself, but shalt perform unto the Lord thine oaths: ³⁴But I say unto you, Swear not at all; neither by heaven; for it is God's throne: ³⁵Nor by the earth; for it is his footstool: neither by Jerusalem; for it is the city of the great King. ³⁶Neither shalt thou swear by thy head, because thou canst not make one hair white or black. ³⁷But let your communication be, Yea, yea; Nay, nay: for whatsoever is more than these cometh of evil. ³⁸**Ye have heard that it hath been said,** An eye for an eye, and a tooth for a tooth: ³⁹But I say unto you, That ye resist not evil: but whosoever shall smite thee on thy right cheek, turn to him the other also. ⁴⁰And if any man will sue thee at the law, and take away thy coat, let him have thy cloak also. ⁴¹ And whosoever shall compel thee to go a mile, go with him twain. ⁴² Give to him that asketh thee, and from him that would borrow of thee turn not thou away. ⁴³ **Ye have heard that it hath been said,** Thou shalt love thy neighbour, and hate thine enemy. ⁴⁴ But I say unto you, Love your enemies, bless them that curse you, do good to them that hate you, and pray for them which despitefully use you, and persecute you; ⁴⁵ That ye may be the children of your Father which is in heaven: for he maketh his sun to rise on the evil and on the good, and sendeth rain on the just and on the unjust. ⁴⁶ For if ye love them which love you, what reward have ye? do not even the publicans the same? ⁴⁷ And if ye salute your brethren only, what do ye more than others? do not even the publicans so? ⁴⁸ **Be ye therefore perfect, even as your Father which is in heaven is perfect.**

Summary

When we say that Christians are not "under the Law," we mean that the ceremonial laws associated with the temple in Jerusalem have ceased. Jesus replaced the temple with His body; by *His* stripes we are healed and cleansed. We no longer need to be ceremonially and ritually cleansed in order to be accepted by God. However, we are still under the moral law, and yet the standards for us are even *stricter* than they were in the Mosaic Law. Even sinning with one's eyes or one's mind is breaking the law! So how do we stand a chance, then? The good news is that, through faith, we are covered by the blood of the Lamb, and thereby we are made righteous by His righteousness. But that is not the end of the story; it's only the beginning. We must also bear good fruit, do good works, and shun evil deeds. The authentic Christian life is one of obedience, discipline, and service.

NOTES:

We Must Be Known by Our Good Fruits

The difference between good fruits and good works is that "fruits" have more to do with our behavior and character, whereas works have more to do with our deeds.

The mark of a Christian is that we bring forth holy fruit in our lives. Other people recognize us as Christians by our demeanor, by the way we act, and by the way we communicate with others. Our good fruit makes Christ attractive to the world, by our example, and thus helps save souls. A "Christian" with bad fruit is even worse than a non-Christian with bad fruit, because they scandalize the faithful and repel others from Christ and the Church.

We must bear good fruit as "ambassadors for Christ" (2 Corinthians 5:20); we should never, as a result of our rottenness, be the reason why others want nothing to do with Him. We have the free will to produce rotten fruit or good fruit. Whichever way we choose, we will have to give an account to God, so choose wisely!

You Will "Know Them by Their Fruits" (Whether Good or Evil)

- **Matthew 3 [John the Baptist Speaking]:** ¹⁰ And now also the axe is laid unto the root of the trees: therefore **every tree which bringeth not forth good fruit is hewn down, and cast into the fire.**
- **Matthew 7 [Jesus speaking]:** ¹⁵ Beware of false prophets, which come to you in sheep's clothing, but inwardly they are ravening wolves. ¹⁶ **Ye shall know them by their fruits.** Do men gather grapes of thorns, or figs of thistles? ¹⁷ Even so every good tree bringeth forth good fruit; but a corrupt tree bringeth forth evil fruit.

The Works of the Flesh vs. the Fruit of the Spirit

Likewise, a Christian is known by whether they are showing forth the fruit of the Spirit or engaging in the works of the flesh. God expects every born again Christian to produce the fruits of the Spirit in their daily lives.

- **Galatians 5:** ¹⁸ But if ye be led of the Spirit, ye are not under the law. ¹⁹ Now the **works of the flesh** are manifest, which are these; Adultery, fornication, uncleanness, lasciviousness, ²⁰ Idolatry, witchcraft, hatred, variance, emulations, wrath, strife, seditions, heresies, ²¹ Envyings, murders, drunkenness, revellings, and such like: of the which I tell you before, as I have also told you in time past, that they which do such things shall not inherit the kingdom of God. ²² **But the fruit of the Spirit is love, joy, peace, longsuffering, gentleness, goodness, faith,** ²³ **Meekness, temperance: against such there is no law.** ²⁴ And they that are Christ's have crucified the flesh with the affections and lusts. ²⁵ If we live in the Spirit, let us also walk in the Spirit. ²⁶ Let us not be desirous of vain glory, provoking one another, envying one another.
- **Mark 7:** ¹⁸ And he saith unto them, Are ye so without understanding also? Do ye not perceive, that whatsoever thing from without entereth into the man, it cannot defile him; ¹⁹ Because it entereth not into his heart, but into

the belly, and goeth out into the draught, purging all meats? **²⁰ And he said, That which cometh out of the man, that defileth the man.** ²¹ For from within, out of the heart of men, proceed evil thoughts, adulteries, fornications, murders, ²² Thefts, covetousness, wickedness, deceit, lasciviousness, an evil eye, blasphemy, pride, foolishness: ²³ All these evil things come from within, and defile the man.

Summary

The good news of the gospel is meant to be shared, like a banquet of food. When we produce good fruit in our lives, we are actually evangelizing without preaching. We are Christ's ambassadors, and our good behavior benefits everyone around us: by setting an example, we attract others to Christ and help save souls. The fruit of the Spirit is love, joy, peace, longsuffering, gentleness, goodness, faith, meekness, and temperance—the same traits that Christ had.

NOTES:

NOTES:

We Must Fight the Good Fight

The Bible makes it clear that we must have something to show for our faith. It's not enough to simply "believe"—there is a prize to be won, and we must fight for it with all our might.

Athletes and Soldiers

We must approach this Christian life as though we are athletes or soldiers—two metaphors that the Apostle Paul uses to help us understand that the Christian life is not "set it and forget it": Every day we strive for perfection, and we keep our eyes fixed on heaven; we never know if today will be our last day and if today we will need to meet our maker. Therefore, "give diligence to make your calling and election sure" (2 Peter 1:10).

- **1 Corinthians 9:** [24] Know ye not that they which run in a race run all, but **one receiveth the prize?** So run, that ye may obtain. [25] And every man that striveth for the mastery is temperate in all things. Now they do it to obtain a corruptible crown; but we an incorruptible. ²⁶ I therefore so run, not as uncertainly; so **fight I,** not as one that beateth the air: ²⁷ **But I keep under my body, and bring it into subjection:** lest that by any means, when I have preached to others, I myself should be a castaway.

- **Ephesians 6:** ¹⁰ Finally, my brethren, be strong in the Lord, and in the power of his might. ¹¹ **Put on the whole armour of God, that ye may be able to stand against the wiles of the devil.** ¹² **For we wrestle** not against flesh and blood, but against principalities, against powers, against the rulers of the darkness of this world, against spiritual wickedness in high places. ¹³ Wherefore take unto you the whole armour of God, that ye may be able to withstand in the evil day, and having done all, to stand. ¹⁴ Stand therefore, having your loins girt about with truth, and having on the breastplate of righteousness; ¹⁵ And your feet shod with the preparation of the gospel of peace; ¹⁶ Above all, taking the shield of faith, wherewith ye shall be able to quench all the fiery darts of the wicked. [17] And take the helmet of salvation, and the sword of the Spirit, which is the word of God: [18] Praying always with all prayer and supplication in the Spirit, and watching thereunto with all perseverance and supplication for all saints.

Summary

The Christian life is described as a race of athletes, or a battlefield in which we are equipped to fight "principalities and powers" and "wickedness in dark places." We must never be complacent, thinking that since "Jesus paid it all," we can just do and think whatever is convenient and feels good. Jesus said he wants us to be either hot or cold, but the lukewarm he will "spue," or vomit, out of His mouth (Revelation 3:16). No prizefighter or warrior sits around getting flabby and weak: Rather, he trains and punishes his body day and night, tolerating extreme conditions and hardships, and toughening himself for fighting. Our battle is mainly spiritual and invisible: That's why it's called spiritual warfare.

NOTES:

Faith Is Justified by Works

Here is a puzzle: We cannot be saved by our own works (for we are saved by grace), but at the same time, without works our faith is dead (James 2:26). A dead faith is basically no faith at all, just as a corpse can't do anything but rot in the ground. Christians have been grappling with the relationship between faith and works for two millennia. How can we understand it?

The basic question is this: Is it *enough* for a Christian just to "have faith"? No, because even Lucifer and the fallen angels (demons) have "faith" in a certain sense: They all know that God is God, that Christ is the Savior of the world, that both heaven and hell exist, and so forth. So they all have faith in the form of *intellectual assent,* but this assent includes neither love nor obedience, and so it has no salvific merit whatsoever. Demonic "faith" is nothing but fear.

- **James 2:** [18] Yea, a man may say, Thou hast faith, and I have works: shew me thy faith without thy works, and I will shew thee my faith by my works.
  [19] Thou believest that there is one God; thou doest well: **the devils also**

believe, and tremble. ²⁰ But wilt thou know, O vain man, that faith without works is dead? ²¹ Was not Abraham our father justified by works, when he had offered Isaac his son upon the altar? ²² Seest thou how faith wrought with his works, and by works was faith made perfect? ²³ And the scripture was fulfilled which saith, Abraham believed God, and it was imputed unto him for righteousness: and he was called the Friend of God. ²⁴ Ye see then how that **by works a man is justified, and not by faith only.** ²⁵ Likewise also was not Rahab the harlot justified by works, when she had received the messengers, and had sent them out another way? ²⁶ **For as the body without the spirit is dead, so faith without works is dead also.**

However those who live in the Spirit, as manifested by the fruits of the Spirit, naturally operate in the Spirit and will therefore readily, out of a sense of sincere love and obedience, perform good works.

Since the first and great commandment is "Thou shalt love the Lord thy God with all thy heart, and with all they soul, and with all thy mind" and the second, similarly, is "Thou shalt love thy neighbor as thyself," we can know that all good works will be acts of love toward either God or neighbor, or both.

We were created to do good works:

- **Ephesians 2:** [10] For we are his workmanship, **created in Christ Jesus unto good works,** which God hath before ordained that we should walk in them.

We are commanded to do good works because they benefit others:

- **Matthew 5:** [14] Ye are the light of the world. A city that is set on an hill cannot be hid. [15] Neither do men light a candle, and put it under a bushel, but on a candlestick; and it giveth light unto all that are in the house. [16] Let your light so shine before men, **that they may see your good works, and glorify your Father which is in heaven**.
- **Titus 3:** [8] This is a faithful saying, and these things I will that thou affirm constantly, **that they which have believed in God might be careful to maintain good works. These things**

are good and profitable unto men. ⁹But avoid foolish questions, and genealogies, and contentions, and strivings about the law; for they are unprofitable and vain. ¹⁰A man that is an heretick after the first and second admonition reject; ¹¹Knowing that he that is such is subverted, and sinneth, being condemned of himself.

Through the Holy Scriptures, the perfect man is furnished to do good works:

- **2 Timothy 3:** ¹⁶All scripture is given by inspiration of God, and is profitable for doctrine, for reproof, for correction, for instruction in righteousness: ¹⁷That the man of God may be perfect, **thoroughly furnished unto all good works.**

Summary

We cannot be saved by our own good deeds but can only be saved through the grace of God through Christ Jesus and the power of the Holy Spirit, enlivening us to *want* to do good works. Good works are the *evidence* that we are indeed saved; they are not the *means* by which we are saved.

NOTES:

NOTES:

We Go to Church Regularly

Christian Worship Occurs on Sunday

Christians attend church services on Sunday as a way of following the model of the first Church communities. These communities did not gather together on the seventh (Sabbath) day, but rather on the *first* day of the week, which we know as Sunday, to honor the day of Jesus's Resurrection. In a sense, Christians can consider every Sunday to be a "mini Easter"!

- **Luke 24:** [1] Now upon **the first day of the week,** very early in the morning, they came unto the sepulchre, bringing the spices which they had prepared, and certain others with them. [2] And they found the stone rolled away from the sepulchre. [3] And they entered in, and found not the body of the Lord Jesus.
- **Acts 20:** [7] And upon the **first day of the week, when the disciples came together** to break bread, Paul preached unto them, ready to depart on the morrow; and continued his speech

until midnight. ⁸ And there were many lights in the upper chamber, where they were gathered together.

Christians are sternly commanded to gather together to worship and not to forsake it:

- **Hebrews 10:** ²³ Let us hold fast the profession of our faith without wavering; (for he is faithful that promised;) ²⁴ And let us consider one another to provoke unto love and to good works: ²⁵ **Not forsaking the assembling of ourselves together, as the manner of some is;** but exhorting one another: and so much the more, as ye see the day approaching.

Jesus is the Lord of the Sabbath:

- **Matthew 12:** ⁷ But if ye had known what this meaneth, I will have mercy, and not sacrifice, ye would not have condemned the guiltless. ⁸ **For the Son of man is Lord even of the Sabbath day.** ⁹ And when he was departed thence, he went into their synagogue: ¹⁰ And, behold, there was a man which had his hand withered. And they asked him, saying, Is it lawful to heal on the Sabbath days? that they might accuse him. ¹¹ And he said unto them, What man shall there be among you, that shall have one sheep, and if it fall into a pit on the Sabbath day, will he not lay hold on it, and lift it out? ¹² How much then is a man better than a sheep? Wherefore it is lawful to do well on the Sabbath days.

Summary

Just as Jesus is our High Priest and His body is the true Temple, so too is Jesus our Sabbath. Christians do not observe the seventh-day (Saturday) Sabbath, as such observance falls under the Old Covenant. In observance of the Resurrection, the original Christians gathered together on the first day of the week—Sunday—and Christians still do to this day. Thus, every Sunday is a "little Easter" for Christian followers of the Risen Lord. Christians are expected to attend church on Sunday, barring some extenuating circumstance that should be discussed with one's pastor or priest.

NOTES:

We Commune With the Saints

What Does "Saint" Mean?

The word saint simply means "holy one," and "holy" simply means "set apart." Saints are not only those holy ones who have died and are now in heaven (or only certain special Christians who have been canonized by certain churches as saints), but also those who are living on the earth even now, who are doing God's work and have kept themselves set apart. "Pure religion and undefiled before God and the Father is this, To visit the fatherless and widows in their affliction, and to **keep himself unspotted from the world**" (James 1:27).

The Apostles Wrote Letters to *Living* Saints

- **Ephesians 1:** [1] Paul, an apostle of Jesus Christ by the will of God, **to the saints which are at Ephesus,** and to the faithful in Christ Jesus: [2] Grace be to you, and peace, from God our Father, and from the Lord Jesus Christ. [3] Blessed be the God and Father of our

Lord Jesus Christ, who hath blessed us with all spiritual blessings in heavenly places in Christ: ⁴According as he hath chosen us in him before the foundation of the world, that **we should be holy and without blame before him in love**: ⁵Having predestinated us unto the adoption of children by Jesus Christ to himself, according to the good pleasure of his will, ⁶To the praise of the glory of his grace, wherein he hath made us accepted in the beloved.

The Saints Are Also in Heaven

- **Psalm 116:** ¹⁵Precious in the sight of the Lord is the death of his saints. ¹⁶
- **Hebrews 12:** ¹Wherefore seeing we also are **compassed about with so great a cloud of witnesses,** let us lay aside every weight, and the sin which doth so easily beset us, and let us run with patience the race that is set before us, ²Looking unto Jesus the author and finisher of our faith; who for the joy that was set before him endured the cross, despising the

shame, and is set down at the right hand of the throne of God.

- **Revelation 7:** ¹³ And one of the elders answered, saying unto me, What are these which are arrayed in white robes? and whence came they? ¹⁴ And I said unto him, Sir, thou knowest. And he said to me, **These are they which came out of great tribulation, and have washed their robes, and made them white in the blood of the Lamb.** ¹⁵ Therefore are they before the throne of God, and serve him day and night in his temple: and he that sitteth on the throne shall dwell among them.

- **Revelation 19:** ⁷ Let us be glad and rejoice, and give honour to him: for the marriage of the Lamb is come, and his wife hath made herself ready. ⁸ **And to her was granted that she should be arrayed in fine linen, clean and white: for the fine linen is the righteousness of saints.** ⁹ And he saith unto me, Write, Blessed are they which are called unto the marriage supper of the Lamb. And he saith unto me, These are the true sayings of God.

- **In the Apostles' Creed we confess:** "I believe in the Holy Ghost: The holy

Catholic Church; **The Communion of Saints:** The Forgiveness of sins: The Resurrection of the body: And the Life everlasting. Amen.

Practically speaking, what does it mean for a Christian to believe in the "Communion of Saints"? It means we believe that we should have a deep and abiding *agape* love for our fellow Christians—both those who are alive and those who have died in the faith (also known as the "faithful departed").

We do good works both with and for our fellow Christian saints (and even for those who are outside of the Church); we support the widows, the orphans, and the poor in our Christian communities. Likewise, we read about the lives of the saints, we emulate their virtues, and we venerate them for their holiness.

Some Christians display icons of saints (in addition to icons of Jesus and the Blessed Mother) to keep mindful of their holiness and to inspire us to "endure unto the end" so that we may be saved (Matthew 24:13).

Those saints who have died are not without awareness. They are very much alive! They are now able to see God "face to face," whereas we on earth are only able to see through a "glass, darkly." So the saints are glorified with God in heaven and should hold a special place of veneration in the hearts of all Christians.

- **1 Corinthians 13:** [9] For we know in part, and we prophesy in part. [10] But when that which is perfect is come, then that which is in part shall be done away. [11] When I was a child, I spake as a child, I understood as a child, I thought as a child: but when I became a man, I put away childish things. [12] **For now we see through a glass, darkly; but then face to face: now I know in part; but then shall I know even as also I am known.** [13] And now abideth faith, hope, charity, these three; but the greatest of these is charity.

We Are Allowed to Use Icons as Part of the "Communion of Saints"

The **Council Fathers of the Second Council of Nicaea (787 A.D.)**—also known as the Seventh Ecumenical Council or Nicaea II—ruled that *iconoclasm* (i.e., the hostile idea that holy images known as icons are blasphemous and therefore must be destroyed) is heresy. The following are excerpts from the Council's ruling:

DEFINITION

The one who granted us the light of recognizing him, the one who redeemed us from the darkness of idolatrous insanity, Christ our God, when he took for his bride his holy catholic church, having no blemish or wrinkle, promised he would guard her and assured his holy disciples saying, *I am with you every day until the consummation of this age.* This promise however he made not only to them but also to us, who thanks to them have come to believe in his name. To this gracious offer some people paid no attention, being hoodwinked by the treacherous foe they abandoned the true line of reasoning, and setting themselves against the tradition of the catholic church they faltered in their grasp of the truth. As the proverbial saying puts it, they turned askew the axles of their farm carts and gathered no harvest in their hands. Indeed they had the effrontery to criticise the beauty pleasing to God established in the holy monuments; they were priests in name, but not in reality. They were those of whom God calls out by prophecy, Many pastors have destroyed my vine, they have defiled my portion. For they followed unholy men and trusting to their own frenzies they calumniated the holy church, which Christ our God has espoused to himself, and **they failed to distinguish the holy from the profane, asserting that the icons of our Lord and of his saints were no different from the wooden images of satanic idols.**

Therefore the Lord God, not bearing that what was subject to him should be destroyed by such a corruption, has by his good pleasure summoned us together through the divine diligence and decision of Constantine and Irene, our faithful emperor and empress, we who are those responsible for the priesthood everywhere, in order that the divinely inspired tradition of the catholic church should receive Confirmation by a public decree. So having made investigation with all accuracy and having taken counsel, setting for our aim the truth, we neither *diminish* nor *augment*, but simply *guard* intact all that pertains to the catholic church....

- **Canon 7:** The divine apostle Paul said: The sins of some people are manifest, those of others appear later. Some sins take the front rank but others follow in their footsteps. Thus in the train of the impious heresy of the defamers of Christians, many other impieties appeared. **Just as those heretics removed the sight of venerable icons from the church, they also abandoned other customs, which should now be renewed** and which should be in vigour in virtue of both written and unwritten legislation. Therefore we decree that in venerable churches consecrated without relics of the holy martyrs, the installation of relics should take place along with the usual prayers. And if in future any bishop is found out consecrating a church without relics, let him be

deposed as someone who has flouted the ecclesiastical traditions.
- **Canon 8:** Since some of those who come from the religion of the Hebrews mistakenly think to make a mockery of Christ who is God, pretending to become Christians, but denying Christ in private by both secretly continuing to observe the Sabbath and maintaining other Jewish practices, we decree that they shall not be received to Communion or at prayer or into the church, but rather let them openly be Hebrews according to their own religion; they should not baptize their children or buy, or enter into possession of, a slave. But if one of them makes his conversion with a sincere faith and heart, and pronounces his confession wholeheartedly, disclosing their practices and objects in the hope that others may be refuted and corrected, such a person should be welcomed and baptized along with his children, and **care should be taken that they abandon Hebrew practices.** However if they are not of this sort, they should certainly not be welcomed.

- **Canon 9:** All those childish baubles and bacchic rantings, **the false writings composed against the venerable icons, should be given in at the episcopal building in Constantinople, so that they can be put away along with other heretical books.** If someone is discovered to be hiding such books, if he is a bishop, priest or deacon, let him be suspended, and if he is a lay person or a monk, **let him be excommunicated....**

ANATHEMAS CONCERNING HOLY IMAGES *(Nicaea II, Continued)*

1. If anyone does not *confess* that Christ our God can be represented in his humanity, let him be **anathema**.

2. If anyone does not *accept* representation in art of evangelical scenes, let him be **anathema**.

3. If anyone does not *salute* such representations as standing for the Lord and his saints, let him be **anathema**.

4. If anyone *rejects* any *written or unwritten* tradition of the church, let him be **anathema**.

The Communion of Saints *may* involve the installation of icons in certain churches and the veneration of the saints depicted on those icons. If a Christian is scandalized by this, then that Christian is living in ignorance at best and serious error at worst, since the iconoclast heresy was condemned by the Church Fathers long ago.

Veneration vs. Worship

To the saints, we give veneration only, never worship. The word in Greek for veneration is *doulia* (δουλεία), which literally means "servitude" or "service" or "slavery," meaning we are putting ourselves at the feet of the holy saints, whom we emulate.

The Greek term *hyperdoulia* (ὑπέρ δουλεία) is reserved for the Blessed Virgin alone, since she is above all the saints by virtue of her being the Mother of God. Therefore the highest veneration is due to her.

Finally, the Greek word *latria* (λατρεία) is reserved for God alone. Latria describes the adoration and worship that is due only to the Holy Trinity, who alone as the Godhead is due worship, for "Thou shalt have no other gods before me" (Exodus 20:3).

In traditional apostolic churches, icons of Jesus, Mary, and the saints are very often placed on the altar wall. This placement of the icons serves as a kind of *iconostasis*, especially in humbler churches whose parishioners cannot afford to have an actual *iconostasis* commissioned.

When anyone (priest, deacon, altar boy, reader, acolyte) approaches the altar table, which will have atop it either a cross or a crucifix, the proper form is to bow reverently. In doing so, the icons, the cross, and the altar are venerated as being very holy on the one hand, and God Himself is worshipped properly in His holy house, as it is meet and right to do.

Summary

Icons *are not* the same as idols. Idols represent demonic spirits that pagans call "gods." Icons are more like the images we display of our beloved relatives who have died, since the saints are part of our family in the Communion of Saints. Icons inspire us to holiness and to emulate each saint depicted.

Every Christian is free *not* to use icons, but a Christian **may not forbid** other Christians to use them and venerate them. Veneration can look like bowing, kissing, and adorning the icons. Protestant Christians *do not* pray to saints in order to ask for their intercession. Other Christians (e.g., Roman Catholic, Eastern Orthodox) *do* pray to saints (meaning they talk to them, because they recognize them as being alive in Christ, not dead), but no Christian worships them.

NOTES:

As Saints, We Must Suffer

Our Reward Is Not Here

You may have heard certain pseudo-Christian preachers saying that you can "name it and claim it" and thereby get rich in this life by blasphemously calling on God to increase your wealth. You may have heard certain other false preachers tell you that God wants to you "live your best life now," and that if you are a Christian, you will not only enjoy wealth, but you will also experience health, happiness, longevity, and all the other comforts of life without having to ever suffer. All you have to do is open your wallet and send them "seed money," touch your TV screen, and everything you want for yourself will come true.

These wicked charlatans rake in the cash and fly around on their jet planes from one mansion to the other while duping poorly catechized souls deeper and deeper into their own delusions, never actually evangelizing anyone with the truth of the gospel, but rather exploiting the gullibility and greed of others for purposes of their own cynical lust for money and power.

The road to heaven—to the kingdom of God—is not paved with diamonds and dollars. In fact, Christ said that you cannot serve two masters, that is, both God and money (also called mammon):

- **Matthew 6:** [24] No man can **serve two masters**: for either he will hate the one, and love the other; or else he will hold to the one, and despise the other. Ye cannot **serve** God and mammon.

We Must Take Up Our Cross and Follow Him

Next, Jesus said that we must take up our cross daily and follow Him. This isn't a bland saying at all! Rather, taking up your cross means to be willing to suffer terrible rejection, humiliation, betrayal, torture, and even death, daily, rather than deny Him.

- **Luke 9:** [22] Saying, The Son of man must suffer many things, and be rejected of the elders and chief priests and scribes, and be slain, and be raised the third day. [23] And he said to them all, If any man will come after me, let him deny himself, and **take up his cross daily,** and follow me. [24] For whosoever will save his life shall lose it: but whosoever will lose his life for my sake, the same shall save it.

- **Matthew 10 [Jesus speaking]:** [21] And the brother shall deliver up the brother to death, and the father the child: and the children shall rise up against their parents, and cause them to be put to death. [22] **And ye shall be hated of all men for my name's sake: but he that endureth to the end shall be saved.** [23] But when they persecute you in this city, flee ye into another: for verily I say unto you, Ye shall not have gone over the cities of Israel, till the Son of man be come. [24] The disciple is not above his master, nor the servant above his lord. ... [32] **Whosoever therefore shall confess me before men, him will I confess also before my Father which is in heaven.** [33] **But whosoever shall deny me before men, him will I also deny before my Father which is in heaven.** [34] Think not that I am come to send peace on earth: I came not to send peace, but a sword. [35] For I am come to set a man at variance against his father, and the daughter against her mother, and the daughter in law against her mother in law. ³⁶ And a man's foes shall be they of his own household. ³⁷ **He that loveth father or mother more than me is not worthy of me: and he that loveth son or daughter more than me is not worthy of me.** ³⁸ **And he that taketh not his cross, and followeth after me, is not worthy of me.** ³⁹ **He that findeth his life shall lose it: and he that loseth his life for my sake shall find it.**

- **John 15:** ¹⁹ If ye were of the world, the world would love his own: but because ye are not of the world, but I have chosen you out of the world, **therefore the world hateth you.** ²⁰ Remember the word that I said unto you, The servant is not greater than his lord. **If they have persecuted me, they will also persecute you;** if they have kept my saying, they will keep yours also.
- **1 Peter 4:** ¹² Beloved, think it not strange concerning the fiery trial which is to try you, as though some strange thing happened unto you: ¹³ **But rejoice, inasmuch as ye are partakers of Christ's sufferings; that, when his glory shall be revealed, ye**

may be glad also with exceeding joy. ¹⁴ If ye be reproached for the name of Christ, happy are ye; for the spirit of glory and of God resteth upon you: on their part he is evil spoken of, but on your part he is glorified. ¹⁵ But let none of you suffer as a murderer, or as a thief, or as an evildoer, or as a busybody in other men's matters. ¹⁶ Yet if any man suffer as a Christian, let him not be ashamed; but let him glorify God on this behalf. ¹⁷ For the time is come that judgment must begin at the house of God: and if it first begin at us, what shall the end be of them that obey not the gospel of God? ¹⁸ And if the righteous scarcely be saved, where shall the ungodly and the sinner appear? ¹⁹ **Wherefore let them that suffer according to the will of God commit the keeping of their souls to him in well doing, as unto a faithful Creator.**

We Must Bear One Another's Burdens

It is not even enough to take up our own cross daily and follow Him. If we see others weighed down by anything—whether spiritual or physical—it is our duty to try to help them. That is what is meant by bearing one another's burdens. We can restore their soul by counseling them and encouraging them, and we can also restore their hope serving their physical needs to the best of our ability. In this way, we are being a servant to Christ and a servant to others.

- **Galatians 6:** ¹Brethren, if a man be overtaken in a fault, ye which are spiritual, restore such an one in the spirit of meekness; considering thyself, lest thou also be tempted. ²**Bear ye one another's burdens, and so fulfil the law of Christ…** ⁷Be not deceived; God is not mocked: for whatsoever a man soweth, that shall he also reap. ⁸For he that soweth to his flesh shall of the flesh reap corruption; but he that soweth to the Spirit shall of the Spirit reap life everlasting. ⁹**And let us not be weary in well doing: for**

- **in due season we shall reap, if we faint not.**
- **John 13:** ¹² So after he had washed their feet, and had taken his garments, and was set down again, he said unto them, Know ye what I have done to you? ¹³ Ye call me Master and Lord: and ye say well; for so I am. ¹⁴ **If I then, your Lord and Master, have washed your feet; ye also ought to wash one another's feet.** ¹⁵ **For I have given you an example, that ye should do as I have done to you.** ¹⁶ Verily, verily, I say unto you, The servant is not greater than his lord; neither he that is sent greater than he that sent him.

Summary

To follow Christ means to unite with Him through sufferings, not to be rewarded with the pleasures of the world: "Ye adulterers and adulteresses, know ye not that the friendship of the world is enmity with God? whosoever therefore will be a friend of the world is the enemy of God" (James 4:4). The point of suffering for Christ is to keep our hearts and minds on heaven and not on the material world, which will pass away. The servant is not greater than the master: Our Master willingly suffered and died for us; likewise, we should be willing to suffer for His sake and for the sake of others. For many of us, suffering may look like bullying, betrayal, social rejection, isolation, and the like. All of this persecution and suffering can even lead to unjust imprisonment and martyrdom. Today, people all over the world (Nigeria, Syria, Sudan, etc.) are being tortured and killed daily simply because they are Christians. The purpose of suffering is self-sacrifice in order to epitomize love—"for God is love" (1 John 4:8), and He wants us to be perfect like Him.

NOTES:

NOTES:

Heaven and Hell Are Real

Every Christian is duty-bound to believe that at the point of death, a person's spirit faces judgment—either that person will meet Jesus in heaven, or that person *will not.*

There's a lack of consensus in the Christian world regarding the "will not" part of this statement. Will the Christian with unrepented/unabsolved sins go into a state of Purgatory (Roman Catholic) or through a series of aerial toll houses (Eastern Orthodox) before finally reaching heaven? Will the wicked, unsaved person's spirit immediately experience hellfire, or will that spirit go to some dark and shadowy place forever, or until the Last Judgment?

Jesus Describes Two Types of Hell

Outer Darkness

- **Matthew 8:** [11] And I say unto you, That many shall come from the east and west, and shall sit down with Abraham, and Isaac, and Jacob, in the kingdom of heaven. [12] But the children of the kingdom shall be cast out into **outer**

darkness: there shall be weeping and gnashing of teeth.

Unquenchable Fire, Eternal Corruption

- **Mark 9:** [42] And whosoever shall offend one of these little ones that believe in me, it is better for him that a millstone were hanged about his neck, and he were cast into the sea. [43] And if thy hand offend thee, cut it off: it is better for thee to enter into life maimed, than having two hands to **go into hell,** into the fire that never shall be quenched: [44] **Where their worm dieth not, and the fire is not quenched.** [45] And if thy foot offend thee, cut it off: it is better for thee to enter halt into life, than having two feet to be cast into hell, into the fire that never shall be quenched: [46] Where their worm dieth not, and the fire is not quenched.

We don't know exactly what hell will look like for each unsaved person, or whether there may even possibly be multiple layers of heaven and hell. We have all heard expressions like "the seventh heaven" and "the lowest circle of hell," so we all seem to have a sense that there may be a rich complexity to these two sides of the afterlife—one positive, one negative.

But we do know this, and we must believe it to be true: Jesus has prepared a place for us in heaven, and for a Christian, to be absent from the body is to be present with the Lord.

- **John 14 [Jesus speaking]:** ¹ Let not your heart be troubled: ye believe in God, believe also in me. ² In my Father's house are many mansions: if it were not so, I would have told you. **I go to prepare a place for you.** ³ And if I go and prepare a place for you, I will come again, and receive you unto myself; that where I am, there ye may be also.
- **2 Corinthians 5:** ¹ For we know that if our earthly house of this tabernacle were dissolved, we have a building of God, an house not made with hands, eternal in the heavens. ² For in this we groan, earnestly desiring to be clothed upon with our house which is from heaven: ³ If so be that being clothed we shall not be found naked. ⁴ For we that are in this tabernacle do groan, being burdened: not for that we would be unclothed, but clothed upon, that

mortality might be swallowed up of life. ⁵ Now he that hath wrought us for the selfsame thing is God, who also hath given unto us the earnest of the Spirit. ⁶ **Therefore we are always confident, knowing that, whilst we are at home in the body, we are absent from the Lord:** ⁷ **(For we walk by faith, not by sight:)** ⁸ **We are confident, I say, and willing rather to be absent from the body, and to be present with the Lord.** ⁹ Wherefore we labour, that, whether present or absent, we may be accepted of him. ¹⁰ For we must all appear before the judgment seat of Christ; that every one may receive the things done in his body, according to that he hath done, whether it be good or bad.

The Danger of Mortal Sin

The worst thing we could ever hear after we die is Jesus saying to us, "I never knew you: depart from me":

- **Matthew 7:** ²¹ Not every one that saith unto me, Lord, Lord, shall enter into the kingdom of heaven; but he that doeth the will of my Father which is in heaven. ²² Many will say to me in that day, Lord, Lord, have we not prophesied in thy name? and in thy name have cast out devils? and in thy name done many wonderful works? ²³ And then will I profess unto them, **I never knew you: depart from me, ye that work iniquity.**

Notice that Jesus is saying this to people who *think* they are Christians but are actually deceived. These are people who "work iniquity" despite their good deeds. What are the iniquitous things that a "Christian" may engage in that would bar them from entrance into heaven?

- **1 Corinthians 6:** ⁹ Know ye not that the unrighteous shall not inherit the kingdom of God? **Be not deceived: neither fornicators, nor idolaters, nor adulterers, nor effeminate, nor abusers of themselves with mankind, ¹⁰ Nor thieves, nor covetous, nor drunkards, nor revilers, nor extortioners, shall inherit the kingdom of God.** ¹¹ And such were some of you: but ye are washed, but ye are sanctified, but ye are justified in the name of the Lord Jesus, and by the

Spirit of our God. ...[18] Flee fornication. Every sin that a man doeth is without the body; but he that committeth fornication sinneth against his own body.

- **Galatians 5:21** [19] Now the works of the flesh are manifest, which are these; **Adultery, fornication, uncleanness, lasciviousness,** [20] **Idolatry, witchcraft, hatred, variance, emulations, wrath, strife, seditions, heresies,** [21] **Envyings, murders, drunkenness, revellings, and such like:** of the which I tell you before, as I have also told you in time past, that they which do such things shall not inherit the kingdom of God.
- **Revelation 21:** [7] He that overcometh shall inherit all things; and I will be his God, and he shall be my son. [8] But the **fearful, and unbelieving, and the abominable, and murderers, and whoremongers, and sorcerers, and idolaters, and all liars,** shall have their part in the lake which burneth with fire and brimstone: which is the second death.

While it is true that we cannot *gain heaven* by doing good works, it is also true that we *can lose heaven* by engaging in works of iniquity—irrespective of what we believe.

Young people today are bombarded daily with filthy images and music lyrics, leading to temptations toward pride, lust, violence, greed, and so on—most especially through their handheld devices. It's critical for young people to put on the "whole armor of God" in order to withstand these daily temptations so that they "may stand against the wiles of the devil" (Ephesians 6:11) and not be disqualified from entering into the kingdom of God (1 Corinthians 9:27).

Summary

Heaven and hell are real, and they must be taken seriously. The Psalmist implores God, "teach us to number our days, that we may apply our hearts unto wisdom" (Psalm 90:12). This prayer asks God to keep us mindful that one day we will die. Lucifer and all the fallen angels meanwhile try to tempt us with worldly things and distract us with vanities so that we will keep our minds on anything *except* our final end. The wicked do not just disappear when they die (that's the annihilationist heresy). They face eternal separation from God: That separation might look like a dreadful and dark place filled with weeping and gnashing of teeth, or it might look like hellfire. Christians must prepare to be with Jesus after we die. Jesus has prepared a place for us already, and to attain the prize of heaven, we must beat our bodies "into subjection" (1 Corinthians 9:27) and stay ever sober, ever vigilant, until we breathe our last. We have confidence that whoever "shall endure unto the end" shall be saved (Matthew 24:13).

NOTES:

NOTES:

We Believe in the Life of the World to Come

The Lord's Prayer is probably the most foundational of all Christian prayers. Every Christian child is brought up to know the Lord's Prayer by heart, and Christians pray this prayer every Sunday during Mass as well. The Lord's Prayer is very short, but it is full of references to a future "world to come." The "world to come" is *on earth*, and it refers to the kingdom of God, not heaven.

- **Matthew 6:** [9] After this manner therefore pray ye: Our Father which art in heaven, Hallowed be thy name. [10] **Thy kingdom come, Thy will be done in earth,** as it is in heaven. [11] Give us this day our daily bread. [12] And forgive us our debts, as we forgive our debtors. [13] And lead us not into temptation, but deliver us from evil: **For thine is the kingdom,** and the power, and the glory, for ever. Amen.
- In the **Nicene Creed** we confess: "And I look for the Resurrection of the dead: **And the Life of the world to come. Amen.**"

A New Heaven and a New Earth

At the Second Coming of Our Lord, the wicked will be destroyed and a new heaven and new earth will be established. Only then will God's "kingdom come" and His "will be done in the earth":

- **2 Peter 3:** [10] But the day of the Lord will come as a thief in the night; in the which **the heavens shall pass away with a great noise, and the elements shall melt with fervent heat, the earth also and the works that are therein shall be burned up.** [11] Seeing then that all these things shall be dissolved, what manner of persons ought ye to be in all holy conversation and godliness, [12] Looking for and hasting unto the coming of the day of God, wherein the heavens being on fire shall be dissolved, and the elements shall melt with fervent heat? [13] **Nevertheless we, according to his promise, look for new heavens and a new earth, wherein dwelleth righteousness.**

In this kingdom of God, also known as the Millennial Kingdom, which will be ruled by Christ Himself over the nations, righteousness will dwell for a thousand years—but there will still be a gulf fixed between heaven and earth during this time:

- **Revelation 20:** ¹ And I saw an angel come down from heaven, having the key of the bottomless pit and a great chain in his hand. ² And he laid hold on the dragon, that old serpent, which is the Devil, and Satan, and bound him a thousand years, ³ And cast him into the bottomless pit, and shut him up, and set a seal upon him, that he should deceive the nations no more, **till the thousand years should be fulfilled:** and after that he must be loosed a little season.

Finally, after this kingdom of God on earth, there will be eternity itself: the point when heaven and earth are consummated into one, like a bridegroom with his bride on their wedding day. Heaven **will come down to earth,** and they will combine together in eternal bliss, where there will be no more sorrow, or sickness, or war, or sin, or any such thing—only eternal joy! This is the ultimate "Life of the world to come," the New Jerusalem, which we all hope for:

- **Revelation 21:** ¹ And I saw a new heaven and a new earth: for the first heaven and the first earth were passed away; and there was no more sea. ² **And I John saw the holy city, new Jerusalem, coming down from God out of heaven, prepared as a bride adorned for her husband.** ³ And I heard a great voice out of heaven saying, Behold, the tabernacle of God is with men, and he will dwell with them, and they shall be his people, and God himself shall be with them, and be their God. ⁴ And God shall wipe away all tears from their eyes; and there shall be no more death, neither sorrow, nor crying, neither shall there be any more pain: for the former things are passed away. ⁵ And he that sat upon the throne said, Behold, I make all things new. And he said unto me, Write: for these words are true and faithful. ⁶ And he said unto me, It is done. I am Alpha and Omega, the beginning and the end. I will give unto him that is athirst of the fountain of the water of life freely. ⁷He that overcometh shall inherit all things; and I will be his God, and he shall be my son.

Summary

Although there is certainly much beauty in the created (though fallen) world even today, this world will one day pass away. We must believe in and look forward to the "Life of the world to come" because that new heaven and new earth are part of the divine plan to bring us back to Paradise, where we will live in peace and love with God forever. May we all see the kingdom of God one day and thereafter live in the New Jerusalem for all eternity. Amen.

www.ingramcontent.com/pod-product-compliance
Lightning Source LLC
Chambersburg PA
CBHW050517100526
44581CB00001B/15